INTERACTIVE STORYTELLING

Keith Park

INTERACTIVE STORYTELLING

Developing Inclusive Stories for Children and Adults

SECOND EDITION

www.speechmark.net

First published in 2004 by
Speechmark Publishing Ltd, 70 Alston Drive, Bradwell Abbey, Milton Keynes MK13 9HG, UK
Tel: +44 (0) 1908 326 944 Fax: +44 (0) 1908 326 960
www.speechmark.net

002-5733/Printed in the United Kingdom by CMP (UK)

British Library Cataloguing in Publication Data
Park, Keith
  Interactive storytelling : developing inclusive stories for children & adults
  1. Storytelling – Therapeutic use   2. Learning disabilities – Treatment
  I. Title
  616.8'588906516

ISBN 978 0 86388 819 9

Contents

Acknowledgements

Alice Gallimore, the staff of Globe Education at Shakespeare's Globe Theatre, the staff and pupils of Greenvale School, Nicola Grove, the staff of William C Harvey School, Joyce James, Christina Maloney, BJ Martin, Marie Savill, Kay Wallace, and Doreen and Petrea Woolard.

I would particularly like to thank Nevin Gouda for her advice and guidance in Arabic language and culture, for her collaboration in the preparation of the *Othello* and *Bir Atallah* scripts, and for teaching me how to send text messages in Arabic.

Introduction

Interactive storytelling in practice and theory

'Meat of the Tongue', a Swahili story from Angela Carter's collection of fairy tales (Carter, 1991), tells of a sultan whose unhappy wife grows leaner and more listless every day. The sultan sees a poor man whose wife is healthy and happy, and he asks the poor man his secret. 'Very simple,' answers the poor man, 'I feed her meat of the tongue.' The sultan immediately orders the butcher to buy the tongues of all the slaughtered animals of the town, and feeds them to his wife. The queen gets even more thin and poorly. The sultan then orders the poor man to exchange wives. Once in the palace, the poor man's wife grows thin and pale. The final part of the story goes as follows:

> The poor man, after coming home at night, would greet his new (royal) wife, tell her about the things he had seen, especially the funny things, and then tell her stories that made her shriek with laughter. Next he would take his banjo and sing her songs, of which he knew a great many. Until late at night he would play with her and amuse her. And lo! the queen grew fat in a few weeks, beautiful to look at, and her skin was shining and taut, like a young girl's skin. And she was smiling all day, remembering the many funny things her new husband had told her. When the sultan called her back she refused to come. So the sultan came to fetch her, and found her all changed and happy. He asked her what the poor man had done to her, and she told him. Then he understood the meaning of meat of the tongue. (Carter, 1991, p215)

Storytelling, it seems, is a vital ingredient of human experience. But how can we do the activity of storytelling in a way that will include people who have sensory impairments and additional disabilities? Why should we bother? Jean Ware provides an answer when she suggests that, when choosing activities for children with profound and multiple learning difficulties, our aim should be 'to enable the child to participate in those experiences which are uniquely human' (Ware, 1994, p72). Storytelling may be one of these uniquely human experiences. Whether it is legend, myth, folk-tale, fairy-story, poem, novel, film or play, the principle is the same: everyone everywhere enjoys stories. According to the story 'Meat of the Tongue', we all need them.

Interactive storytelling, as described in this book, began as a way of including children and adults with the most severe and profound learning disabilties in storytelling activities. The method used with all of the stories is 'call and response'. This approach is many thousands of years old, and is still used in various forms throughout the world – notably in British pantomime, which uses a noisy 'call and response' technique in narrating favourite fairy-tales for an appreciative theatre audience over the Christmas season.

In 'call and response' the storyteller calls out a line, and the other participants respond either by repeating the same words or by calling out a different line, and so on throughout the story. This rhythmic exchange between the storyteller and the group provides a powerful momentum. It is very simple, very effective, and very enjoyable. However, it soon became apparent that the same methods of storytelling, and the same storytelling content, could be used with people with or without learning disabilities. Some of the stories contained in this book have been used in a wide range of settings, irrespective of disability.

This book first describes the principles of interactive storytelling, and then gives some practical hints on how to get started. The rest of the book provides a number of different story scripts – ranging from pantomime, poetry and folk-tales from around the world to Shakespeare, Dickens and *Beowulf* – all of which can be done with few or no props, and at almost no cost.

PRINCIPLES OF INTERACTIVE STORYTELLING

The principles of interactive storytelling reflect the fact that its initial development was with groups of children or adults with severe and profound learning disabilities. Nevertheless, they apply equally to all of us, irrespective of disability.

1 The music of words: apprehension precedes comprehension

Oscar Wilde has one of his characters make a joke in the play *An Ideal Husband*, saying that he never goes to Strauss concerts because the music is always in German. It may be an instructive joke: if we can all enjoy the guitar and piano music, why can we not all enjoy the music of words? Song, poetry and prose all contain the music of the human voice, and can be experienced and enjoyed by everyone, whether or not they are able to decode, or re-phrase – a process that often passes for understanding – the meaning of the author or composer.

Introducing their adaptation of Homer's *Odyssey* for individuals with severe and profound learning disabilities, Grove and Park (1996) ask:

> How necessary is verbal comprehension to the understanding of poetry and literature? We know that people with profound learning disabilities can enjoy music, so why not the music of words? Do we have to comprehend before we can apprehend? Does the meaning of a poem or story have to be retrieved through a process of decoding individual words, or can it be grasped through a kind of atmosphere created through sound and vision?

A good illustration of this 'atmosphere created through sound and vision' is provided by Samuel Taylor Coleridge's *Kubla Khan* – a lyrical poem of some 70 lines whose precise subject matter has been a matter of conjecture since its publication in 1798. The poet and critic Swinburne, a contemporary of Dickens, once described the poem as being the supreme example of music in the English language. Here are the final nine lines of *Kubla Khan*. They begin with a reference to the 'stately pleasure dome' decreed by Kubla Khan at the beginning of the poem:

> I would build that dome in air,
> That sunny dome! Those caves of ice!
> And all who heard should see them there,
> And all should cry, beware! Beware!
> His flashing eyes, his floating hair!
> Weave a circle round him thrice
> And close your eyes with holy dread
> For he on honeydew hath fed
> And drunk the milk of paradise

Swinburne argued that any attempt to analyse this poem would be like trying to unravel a rainbow. It is difficult and perhaps impossible to 'decode' this poem, just as it may be impossible to 'decode' the meaning of music, but, when read aloud, the poem can seem to be a mysterious and magical incantation (readers are recommended to try this).

A second example from twentieth-century literature is *Finnegans Wake*, the monumental novel by James Joyce (1971), the first word of which is 'riverrun'. A circular book with no beginning and no end, the sentence on the last page – 628 – begins 'a way a lone a last a loved a long the', and is then completed by the first words of the first page: 'riverrun, past Eve and Adam's, from swerve of shore to bend of bay...' The last few lines on the final page and the first few lines on the first page therefore read as follows (please note there are no typographical errors in the following extract), in what may be the first and only circular novel:

> End here. Us then. Finn, again! Take. Bussoftlhee, mememormee! Till thousandsthee. Lps.
> The keys to. Given! A way a lone a last a loved a long the/riverrun, past Eve and
> Adam's, from swerve of shore to bend of bay, brings us by a commodius vicus of
> recirculation back to Howth Castle and Environs. (Joyce, 1971, p628; p3)

The storyline of the book is scarily complex; large parts of it are unintelligible, and yet when it is heard it has poetic prose of great beauty and power. The book has been described as unreadable: 'massive, baffling, serving nothing but itself, suggesting a meaning but never quite yielding anything but a fraction of it, and yet...desperately simple' (Burgess, 1982, p185). James Joyce suffered from eye problems all his adult life, and was nearly blind during the 17 years it took him to complete *Finnegans Wake*. Large parts of it were dictated by him in a language that is not really English, but a dream-like combination of many languages. Anthony Burgess playfully suggested that the language of *Finnegans Wake* was 'Pun-European', and concluded: '*Finnegans Wake*... is a terminus for the author – all the trains of his learning end up there – but it is also a starting-point for the reader' (Burgess, 1982, p187). This is a second hint, perhaps, for the reader (or in this case, the hearer) to construct their own meanings.

The following extract from *Finnegans Wake*, constructed out of the last and first sentences of the book, contains a mixture of rhythm and timing that is easy to do, although harder to describe on paper: 'riverrun' is three short beats, while the intervening lines are slower. The music of words should become apparent on reading it aloud. It was successfully used as part of a poetry workshop for teenagers.

> riverrun
> from swerve of shore to bend of bay
> riverrun
> a way a lone a last
> a loved a long the
> riverrun
> from swerve of shore to bend of bay
> riverrun

The poet Ezra Pound, editing his own edition of *Selected Cantos*, approvingly quotes the psychoanalyst Jung: 'Being essentially the instrument for his work he (the artist) is subordinate to it and we have no reason for expecting him to interpret it for us. He has done the best that is in him by giving it form and he must leave interpretation to others and to the future' (Pound, 1965, p9). The writer Samuel Beckett once said of *Finnegans Wake* that 'it isn't about anything – it just *is*'. A first step towards constructing meaning might be to provide opportunities for the apprehension of texts that involves active participation. Instead of just hearing and seeing a piece of literature, we can explore the possibilities of acting it out, and then see how people respond to the experience.

2 To see it feelingly: affect and engagement are central to responses to literature
In her discussion of using literature with individuals with severe and profound learning disabilities, Grove suggests that:

> Meaning is grounded in emotion, or affect, which provides the earliest and most fundamental impulse for communication... It follows that we can take two routes when adapting literature for students with language difficulties. We can build rich affective associations, using stretches of text as script, emphasizing the feel of the meaning. This can be regarded as a 'top-down' approach. The second approach is 'bottom-up', and involves decoding meaning through simplification and explanation. The starting point for the top-down approach is to generate an emotional response to the text (Grove, 1998, pp15–16).

One morning I went into a school to start a workshop on *Macbeth* with a group of
teenagers with severe learning disabilities. We turned off the lights, closed the curtains,
and recited the following lines in a whispered call and response:

> Double, double toil and trouble
> Fire burn and cauldron bubble
> Fillet of a fenny snake
> In the cauldron boil and bake
> Eye of newt and toe of frog
> Wool of bat and tongue of dog
> Adders fork and blind worm's sting
> Lizard leg and howlet's wing
> For a charm of powerful trouble
> Like a hell-broth boil and bubble
> Double double toil and trouble
> Fire burn and cauldron bubble.
> (*Macbeth*, IV.i.10–21)

After the final line one of teenagers shivered and said 'Light on'. So the lights were
switched back on, and her teacher asked her why she wanted the lights back on. 'Scary,'
she replied.

The Egyptian folk-tale *Bir Atallah* is performed using Arabic words and phrases with English
(and, most importantly, was prepared in collaboration with a colleague who speaks Arabic
as a first language). This use of Arabic contributed to the multisensory approach, and many
children and staff have enjoyed the sounds of a foreign language with noises quite unlike
English. The third section, for example, spoken quietly as the animals prepare to go to the
Well of Truth, is followed by everyone shouting out 'Yalla' (let's go!) as quickly as possible:

> Now we must go
> To Atallah
> Bir Atallah
> Well of Truth
> يَلّا يَلّا يَلّا
> *Yalla! Yalla! Yalla! (Let's go!)*

3 To read with the ear: recital and performance are valid means of experiencing stories, drama and poetry

'For most of human history "literature", both fiction and poetry, has been narrated, not
written – heard, not read' (Carter, 1991, pix). Fiction and poetry from around the world
have existed in oral form for many thousands of years, long before the development of

comparatively recent (and more passive) forms: writing, printing, radio, television, cinema, and the internet. The oral narration of stories was, and often still is, a social event where the story is sung, spoken or chanted, or, in other words, performed. Pellowski (1990) describes how the performance of storytelling preceded the written word by many centuries. Storytelling may be far more important than reading and writing: our starting point for literature may therefore be, using Grove's terminology, 'the physicality of text' (Grove, 1998, p11), or, in other words, in performance and recital. Grove also argues that:

> Considering literature as an art form suggests that it can be experienced at a physical level, just like a painting, a piece of music, a film or dance. In the context of a curriculum which consistently emphasizes the exercise of cognition over feeling and imagination, to speak of the physicality of text strikes a radical note. Yet... the appeal of a poem or a story lies in its ability to excite the audience in a way which is first and foremost *sensory*. (Grove, 1998, p11, my emphasis)

WH Gardner, the editor of Hopkins' collected poetry, emphasised that 'Hopkins always insisted that his poems should be read with the ear and not with the eye' (Gardner, 1953, pxxxi). This statement may become clearer after silently reading this extract from Hopkins' poem 'The Windhover', and then reading it aloud:

> I caught this morning morning's minion, king-
> dom of daylight's dauphin, dapple-dawn-drawn Falcon in his riding
> Of the rolling level underneath him steady air, and striding
> High there, how he rung upon the rein of a wimpling wing
> In his ecstasy! then off, off forth on swing,
> As a skate's heel sweeps smooth on a bow-bend: the hurl and gliding
> Rebuffed the big wind. My heart in hiding
> Stirred for a bird, – the achieve of, the mastery of the thing!

In print, the poem may look confusing, but when read aloud it becomes more accessible and even simple – an expression of joy in seeing a bird in flight.

The workshop on *Othello*, performed on stage at Shakespeare's Globe Theatre, uses this principle of 'reading with the ear'. The text is performed trilingually in English, and with phrases from Arabic and British Sign Language (BSL). In activity four, when Othello has become convinced that Desdemona has been unfaithful to him, he says farewell to love and vows revenge. In the workshop, to indicate Othello's emotional torment, we change from English to Arabic and so the text goes as follows (phonetic equivalent of Arabic to the left, Arabic script centre, English translation to the right):

> All my fond love
> Thus do I blow to heaven

Intaha	إنتهى	'Tis gone
Enhud	إنهض	arise
Ya intiquam	يا إنتقام	
Ya aswad	يا أسود	black vengeance!
Hayem wa	هيام و	love and
Intiquam	إنتقام	*vengeance*

In recital, the Arabic used in conjunction with phrases from BSL has an extremely powerful effect. (It is not as difficult as it might sound to use three languages.)

INTERACTIVE STORYTELLING: HOW TO GET STARTED

1 Using call and response

This collection of storytelling activities was originally developed in Greenwich and Lewisham (London) as a means of including children and adults with very high support needs in group activities. Some of the stories, such as 'Red Riding Hood', are clearly for younger children, while others, such as *Othello*, are for teenagers and adults. Several of the stories, such as *Oliver Twist*, 'Snow White' and *A Midsummer Night's Dream*, have been used with groups of children as well as adults.

It has already been mentioned that all the examples of storytelling in this book use the technique of 'call and response'. No special knowledge or expertise is needed to use these stories; they can be performed anywhere with a minimum of equipment. It should be re-emphasised that anyone who wants to try the stories that include words or phrases from another language – for example, Arabic – is recommended to contact a colleague or friend who speaks it as a first language, and who will be able to offer guidance on linguistic and cultural context.

2 Positioning: the circle

This may sound very simple, but we have found that one of the most important aspects of the activities is the position in which participants are arranged. Sitting in a single-line circle formation, with no second row, reinforces group identity and focuses the energy and attention of the participants upon each other. If you try the same activities with everyone arranged in a semicircle formation, you may find, as we did, that it is much harder work, and that the atmosphere and feeling of the group is quite different.

'Drama', WH Auden once suggested, 'began as the act of a whole community. Ideally there would be no spectators.' (Auden, 1977, p273). *Kvad-dansen*, derived from the old Norse word *kvad* meaning 'step', refers to a 'step dance', and is a traditional Scandinavian style of storytelling (Anderson, 1999). Traditionally, the storyteller stands in the middle of the circle calling out the story, while the chorus responds every third or fourth line. This ancient method is still used in some Scandinavian communities, and in particular in the Faroe Islands. WH Auden again:

> ...imagine a circle of people dancing: the circle revolves and comes back to its starting place; at each revolution the set of movements is repeated. When words move in this kind of repeated pattern, we call the effect of the movement in our minds the metre. Words arranged in metre are verse. (Auden, 1977, p307)

In storytelling activities, the group is arranged in a circle, with the group leader in the centre of the circle. The group can then move clockwise or anticlockwise in time to the rhythm of the call and response. Alternatively, instead of moving around in a circle, the participants can move towards the centre of the circle, and then back out again. Most of the poetry in Chapter 4 has been performed in this manner.

3 One-word poetry

This refers to an activity where a single word is chosen – for example, 'everybody' – which is chanted in call and response, and each time one letter is taken away. It is much easier to do than to describe, but this word when chanted would be as follows:

> Everybody-*everybody*
> verybody-*verybody*
> erybody-*erybody*
> rybody-*rybody*
> ybody-*ybody*
> body-*body*
> ody-*ody*
> dy-*dy*
> y- *y*

A particular favourite with some children and staff is the chant of the word 'shampoo':

> Shampoo-*shampoo*
> hampoo-*hampoo*
> ampoo-*ampoo*
> mpoo-*mpoo*
> poo-*poo*
> oo-*oo*
> o-*o!*

One-word name-poetry is a version of the above. This is an introductory exercise to inform all workshop participants who is in the group, and whereabouts in the circle they are situated. The group leader selects a person – for example, Kay, a class teacher – to be the subject of the first poem. This name is chanted in call and response: 'Kay – *Kay*; ay – *ay*; y – *y*' (which of course sounds like: why? why?), followed by a loud cheer to acknowledge Kay. Once again, this is easier to speak than to describe in writing. Next to Kay might be Tony, whose poem would be as follows: 'Tony – *Tony*; ony – *ony*; ny – *ny*; y – *y*', followed by another cheer.

4 Simple poetry

To experiment with speaking poetry aloud in front of a group, it is helpful to start with poems that are easy. *The Magic Pudding* (Lindsay, 1985) is a very famous children's book from Australia, where it was first published in 1918. It tells the adventures of Bunyip Bluegum, Bill Barnacle, Sam Sawnoff and the cantankerous Magic Pudding. The pudding is magic, explains Bill Barnacle, because:

> The more you eat the more you gets. Cut-an'-come-again is his name, an' cut an' come again is his nature. Me an' Sam has been eatin' away at this Puddin' for years, and there's not a mark on him. (Lindsay, 1985, p23)

The 'Song of the Magic Pudding' (Lindsay, 1985, p42), performed using call and response in an extremely grumpy voice, has become a favourite in many schools. This is the first verse:

> Oh who would be a puddin'
> A puddin' in a pot
> A puddin' which is stood in
> A fire which is hot
> O sad indeed the lot
> Of puddin's in a pot.

5 Playing with words

There are many opportunities to play with language and to experiment with contrasts. Try saying words quickly and then slowly, loud and then soft, then quick and loud followed by quietly and softly. Participants may also enjoy changing the emotional register of the words, for example by saying the words sadly, happily, angrily, or as if bored. Another popular way of playing with words is to say them in the style of a famous film star or television personality. Try the 'Magic Pudding' poem in different emotional registers (a manic depressive pudding voice is quite a favourite), and then in the style of John Wayne, Humphrey Bogart, Julian Clary or a Dalek from the long-running 'Dr Who' series. One of the most popular sections of the 'Twelfth Night' workshop for teenagers was when we all tried to speak some of the lines in the style of Peter Sellers as Inspector Clouseau from the 'Pink Panther' series of films.

6 Awareness of rhythm

All of the stories in this collection have strong rhythm, whether they are for children or teenagers and adults. The aspect of rhythm is at least as important as the words themselves. Here are some lines from some of the stories, with the stress in italic type.

For example, the 'Song of the Magic Pudding':

> Oh *who* would *be* a *puddin'*
> A *puddin'* in a *pot*
> A *puddin'* which is *stood in*
> A *fire* which is *hot*
> O *sad* indeed the *lot*
> Of *puddin's* in a *pot*

And the beginning of 'Red Riding Hood':

> I *knock* at the *door*
> Knock, *knock*, knock, *knock*
> She *says* who's *there*
> Who's *there*, who's *there*

Episode two of 'Snow White':

> *You* do the *shop*ping
> *You* cook the *din*ner
> *You* do the *wash*ing up

Episode one of Genesis:

> Joseph *was* the *son* of *Jacob*
> Jacob *dwelt* with*in* the *coun*try
> *Where* his *father was* a *stran*ger

Episode one of *A Midsummer Night's Dream*:

> *What* thou *see'st* when *thou* dost *wake*
> *Do* it *for* thy *true* love *take*

7 Enthusiasm

In the preparation of this book I have asked many people what they think are the most important factors in making a successful storytelling session. Many have answered that staff enthusiasm is the single most important consideration. If you want to use call and response, and the staff as a group are shy and nervous, then you might be in for a difficult time! To begin with, it might be helpful to try some easier activities such as one-word name-poetry as an 'ice-breaker', or a poem with strong rhythm that you already know.

8 Group ownership

Another way to develop staff confidence, as well as your own confidence, is to encourage participation in the story-making process. The story of David and Goliath, in Cockney rhyming slang, had an immediate response in Charlton School (in Greenwich, south-east

London) because many members of staff were familiar with rhyming slang and were keen to make suggestions about alternative phrases. Being keen football supporters, they suggested that the two opposing armies could shout threats in the style of football supporters, so the last two lines are in the style of chanting from the football stadium. (In Cockney rhyming slang, the word 'jack' means 'hill', and the word 'geezer' means 'man'.) See Chapter 3 for an explanation of rhyming slang.

> Israelites over 'ere
> Philistines over there
> Both armies on a jack
> Some geezer called Goliath
> Says 'I'm a Philistine
> Find someone
> To 'ave it out wiv me
> If you fink you're 'ard enough'
> *Come and get it if you fink you're 'ard enough*
> *Oi! Oi! Oi!*

9 Flexibility

The group may develop favourite episodes from some stories. The children who first did 'Red Riding Hood' would do the first episode, which takes only seconds, for up to half an hour at a time. They showed such interest and enjoyment that we all agreed to postpone the second episode until there was a natural break. Similarly, the teenagers who first did 'Jack and the Beanstalk' insisted on repeating the second episode – which ends with everyone yelling 'you know you do my 'ead in' – countless times. After a few sessions of 'Jack and the Beanstalk', one group of teenagers went on to make their own story.

10 Learn the lines

Storytelling sessions are far more likely to be a success if the group leader knows the lines by heart, and does not need to refer to notes. Sometimes it may be necessary to look at a script, but wherever possible it is best to learn the lines before you start. It is also important to feel comfortable with the words – if you are not comfortable with the idea of doing Shakespeare, for example, then it will be much better to try something else. There are plenty of other choices – Spike Milligan's poetry is a great favourite in many schools.

11 Fun

Storytelling activities should be enjoyable. If no one is engaged, think about a change of content, or a change of activity.

12 Communication switches

Several of the people who participated in these storytelling activities are non-speaking and use communication devices. A 'Big Mack', for example, is a single switch, approximately 12 cm in diameter, on to which a single message of up to 20 seconds can be recorded. These switches enable people who are non-speaking to contribute to the activities.

Introduction to the second edition

Since the first edition of this book in 2004 the use of Interactive Storytelling is continuing to develop in three particular ways.

First, inclusion. Many more of the workshops are now inclusive, and this refers to workshops within any particular school, between schools, and similarly between Adult Day Services. One of the most effective projects was one that developed between six special schools. One school visited the five others on a weekly basis, when they would combine with a group from the host school and do some poetry and storytelling in the hall. In the following term, the visits were reversed and the host schools became the visiting schools. This project gave staff and pupils from all the schools the opportunity to see another school and to develop contacts and then exchange ideas.

Second, performances in community venues. A greater emphasis has been placed on performing storytelling activities in a number of community settings. The Shakespeare scripts in this book have been used for performances for the Shakespeare Schools Festival (SSF) and over the last four years, through the invitation of the SSF, pupils from Charlton School have performed Shakespeare at Middle Temple, The National Theatre, BAFTA (the British Academy of Film and Television Awards) and at The House of Commons. We have also been priveliged to be able to perform the Shakespeare workshops on stage at Shakespare's Globe Theatre. The Bible stories have been performed at the church of St Mary-le-Bow, Westminster Abbey, St Paul's Cathedral, Rochester Cathedral and Canterbury Cathedral. And, after I was told that a street performance licence was usually free when performers were not asking for money, pupils have also performed street theatre, using their various scripts in locations in local communities.

Third, and perhaps most significantly, not only staff but pupils have begun to write their own scripts. One pupil with autism, having participated in the 'Cinderella' pantomime, wrote his own interactive script of 'Peter Pan' and then led the workshops on stage at the Churchill Theatre in Bromley (south east London) before performing it with another group of people at Richmond Theatre. He then wrote a script of a Bible story in rhyming slang and was invited to perform it in the nave of Westminster Abbey in front of more than 150 people.

If anyone had told me five years ago that these things would happen, I would not have believed it. So it seems that the only limitations are our own expectations. The additional versions of stories by the Brothers Grimm and Hans Christian Andersen are part of this continuing process. They are being used within schools, and between schools, in a variety of community venues, by both children and adults with and without learning disabilities.

Chapter 1

Folk-tales and Pantomime

Jack and the Beanstalk

This version began as a way to encourage a person called Ben to stay involved in the group activity, and so contains a lot of puns on the word Ben. It has been done by both children and teenagers. The introduction to the story is Episode 1, so it can be started very quickly. The words in italics are the response lines, and the final line of each episode is called out by everyone together. It can be done without any props, although we used a red cloth for the giant to 'get' Jack.

◆ EPISODE 1: INTRODUCTION

This is the story of
Jack and the beanstalk
Jack and the Ben shop?
No! Jack and the beanstalk
Jack and the Ben sock?
No! Jack and the beanstalk
Jack and the Ben talk?
No! Jack and the beanstalk
Alright I heard you
Get on with it!

Activity
The introduction to the activity is part of the activity itself, which means that it can be started very quickly. It also introduces the central idea of mishearing what other people say.

◆ EPISODE 2

Jack and his mother are very poor. Jack's mother tells him to sell their last cow for five... five what?

You got five what?
I got five beans
You got five Bens?
I got five beans
You got five jeans?
I got five beans

You got five queens?
I got five beans!!
You know you do my 'ead in!
Oooohhhh!

Activity

This episode contains more puns on the name Ben, and gets louder and louder until Jack and his mum are so fed up with each other that they shout, at the top of their voices, 'You know you do my 'ead in' in a very over-exaggerated Cockney style, followed by everyone putting their hands on their hips and doing a pantomime-style 'Oooohh!' On many of the occasions when this story has been done, this episode appears to be the favourite.

◆ EPISODE 3

She throws the beans away. The beans talk:

Mung bean?
Mung bean
Soya bean?
Soya bean
Runner bean?
Runner bean
Kidney bean?
Kidney bean
Baked bean?
Baked bean
Has been
Has been
Oh yuk!!

Activity

This episode contains another pantomime-style pun. Several participants of one storytelling group would stand up on the line 'Oh yuk!', and shake their trouser legs!

◆ EPISODE 4

Next day one of the beans is a beanstalk. Jack goes up the beanstalk and meets Mrs Giant; they go to her kitchen and Jack has breakfast. Now the giant is coming; he can smell something strange in the kitchen!

Thump, thump, thump, thump
Thump, thump, thump, thump
Fee-fi-fo-fum
Fee-fi-fo-fum
I smell the blood of an Englishman
I smell the blood of an Englishman
Be he live, or be he dead
Be he live, or be he dead
I'll grind his bones to make my bread
I'll grind his bones to make my bread
You're toast!!
Aarrgghh!

Activity
Everyone stamps loudly in time to the rhythm of the words, and on the line 'You're toast' the giant chooses someone to be the victim, and covers them with the red cloth as everyone screams in mock-horror. As they became familiar with the words of the activity, some teenagers make up their own words, such as 'I smell the blood of an English geezer'; and 'I'll grind his brains to make my bread.'

◆ EPISODE 5

Mrs Giant said:

Never mind dear, it's the bones of the boy that you had for supper. Now settle down and eat your breakfast of:

Three boiled sheep
Three boiled feet?
No! Three boiled sheep
Three royal feet?
No! Three boiled sheep!
Three shredded wheat?
No! Three boiled sheep!
Alright keep your shirt on!
Oooohhhh!

Activity

The call and response is in reverse this time: everyone calls out the first line, and the group leader replies with the misheard response. The exchanges get louder and louder until the final pantomime-style 'Oohh' at the end.

◆ EPISODE 6

The giant falls asleep. Jack takes the hen back down the beanstalk and gives it to his mother. He goes back up the beanstalk and hides in the giant's kitchen. The giant comes in – he can smell something strange in the kitchen!

Thump, thump, thump, thump
Thump, thump, thump, thump
Fee-fi-fo-fum
Fee-fi-fo-fum
I hate boiled sheep
I hate boiled sheep
I want fresh meat
I want fresh meat
He looks tasty
He looks tasty
Let's have a bite
Let's have a bite
Crunch!
Aarrgghh!

Activity

This activity is similar to Episode 4, except here the giant's voice is made to sound very depressed from eating all those sheep until the line 'I want fresh meat', which can be made to sound menacing. The first group to try this story used to enjoy testing visitors by covering them with the red cloth on the line 'Crunch'.

◆ **EPISODE 7**

After another breakfast of three sheep, the giant said to his wife, 'and now bring me my magic harp'. When she did, the giant said:

Sing a song
Bring along?
No! Sing a song
Ping pong?
No! Sing a song!
Ding dong?
No! Sing a song!
Why didn't you say so!
Oooohhhh!

Activity
As in Episode 5, the call and response is in reverse this time: everyone calls out the first line, and the group leader replies with line two, and so on until the loud mock-frustration of the final line.

◆ **EPISODE 8**

The harp sings, and the giant falls asleep. Jack takes the harp, and makes a run for it. The giant chases him down the beanstalk:

Jack chopped the beanstalk
Crunch!
Everybody heard it
Do what?
And that was the end of the giant
Hooray!
And Jack and his mum lived
Happily ever after
Happily ever dafter?
No! Happily ever after
Hooray!

Activity
A boisterous exchange ending with the obligatory 'happily ever after' ending, followed by a loud cheer. For many groups, eight episodes were too many, so they would do three or four episodes, and then 'fast forward' to the final episode to finish.

Cinderella

This is a version of the original Cinderella story by the brothers Grimm (Zipes, 1992), without the Fairy Godmother and Buttons. This story is done in the style of pantomime, and is intended to be colourful and exuberant, and have lots of participation. To encourage the responses ('Booooh!', 'Aaaah!', 'Oh no it isn't!', etc), it might be helpful to have them written on flash-cards shown at the appropriate times. This version is written in verse. Most 'call' lines have eight beats, so that the rhythm drives the storytelling. It was written for a school Christmas show, but has since been enjoyed in a number of settings and with people of all ages. The story is usually done from beginning to end as one episode, but it can be done in smaller episodes, as indicated by the gaps in the text.

Say hello to Cinderella
Hello Cinderella!
Cinderella's ugly sisters
Boooo!
They were off to a three-day party
Ooooh!
Where the prince might find a bride
Aaaah!
'Can I come?' said Cinderella
The ugly sisters said
'You can't go 'cos you can't dance'
You can't go 'cos you can't dance
'You can't go you've got no clothes'
You can't go you've got no clothes
Cinderella went to the hazel tree
She said:
'Shake and shiver little tree'
Shake and shiver, little tree
'Let gold and silver fall on me'
Let gold and silver fall on me
She had a gold and silver dress
She had golden slippers
Cinderella went to the ball
Cinderella danced with the prince
And then she ran back home
Phew!

Day two: the sisters got dressed up
They were off to the three-day party
Ooooh!
Where the prince might find a bride
Aaaah!
'Can I come?' said Cinderella
The ugly sisters said:
'You can't go 'cos you can't dance'
You can't go 'cos you can't dance
'You can't go you've got no clothes'
You can't go you've got no clothes
Cinderella went to the hazel tree
She said:
'Shake and shiver little tree'
Shake and shiver, little tree
'Let gold and silver fall on me'
Let gold and silver fall on me
She had a gold and silver dress
She had golden slippers
She went to the ball
She danced with the prince
And then she ran back home
Phew!

Day three: the sisters got dressed up
They were off to the three-day party
Ooooh!
Where the prince might find a bride
Aaaah!
'Can I come?' said Cinderella
The ugly sisters said:
'You can't go 'cos you can't dance'
You can't go 'cos you can't dance
'You can't go you've got no clothes'
You can't go you've got no clothes
Cinderella went to the hazel tree
She said:
'Shake and shiver little tree'
Shake and shiver, little tree
'Let gold and silver fall on me'
Let gold and silver fall on me
She had a gold and silver dress
She had golden slippers

She went to the ball
She danced with the prince
And then she ran back home
But she had lost her slipper!
Oh No!

The prince picked it up and then he said:
'I'll find the girl whose foot fits this shoe,
And I will marry her'
Aaaahh
He came to Cinderella's house
He said: 'Whose shoe is this?'
The sisters said: 'It's mine, it's mine'
Oh no it isn't!
Oh yes it is!
One sister tried the shoe on;
Her foot's too big, it doesn't fit
Her mother said 'Cut your toe off'
Cut your toe off!
'You won't need it when you're queen'
The two white pigeons said:
'Looky look look at the shoe that she took'
Looky look look at the shoe that she took
'There's blood all over'
Yuk!
'And the shoe's too small'
'She's not the bride you met at the ball'
Oooops!

The other sister tried the shoe on
Her foot's too big, it doesn't fit
Her mother said 'Cut your toe off'
Cut your toe off!
'You won't need it when you're queen'
The two white pigeons said:
'Looky look look at the shoe that she took'
Looky look look at the shoe that she took
'There's blood all over'
Yuk!
'And the shoe's too small'
'She's not the bride you met at the ball'
Oooops!

Cinderella tried the shoe on
[*A long expectant pause here*]
The two white pigeons said:
'Looky look look at the shoe that she took'
Looky look look at the shoe that she took
'The shoe's just right'
'And there's no blood at all'
'She's truly the bride you met at the ball'
Yes!
So Cinderella and the prince got married
Hooray!
And they lived
Happily ever after.

Hansel and Gretel

This version of Hansel and Gretel was written for a group of primary-school aged children. Among other things, it is an introduction to discussing the difference between what people say and what people think – the appearance/reality division that is the theme of so many folk-tales. It is more complex than most of the other stories in this section because the response lines are different from the call lines, so it relies upon the group participants having considerable language skills.

◆ EPISODE 1

Hansel and Gretel are lost in the wood. They come to a strange house made of bread, with cake for a roof and sugar for windows:

> What's the house made of?
> *Bread and cake and sugar*
> What did they say?
> *Let's have a taste*
> What happened next?
> *They nibbled at the house*
> And then, and then they heard this song
> *Nibble, nibble I hear a mouse*
> *Who's that nibbling at my house?*

◆ EPISODE 2

The old woman who lives in the house was singing to them. She invites Hansel and Gretel into the house. The woman is really a wicked witch who cooks children and eats them:

> What did the witch think?
> *Here comes dinner*
> What did the witch say?
> *Please come in*
> What happened next?
> *She crept up to Hansel*
> And then – and then
> *She pushed him in the cage*
> Then slammed the door
> *Bang!*

◆ EPISODE 3

The witch feeds up Hansel to make him more tasty to eat, but Hansel plays a *trick* on the witch:

What did the witch think?
He looks tasty
What did the witch say?
Let me feel
What happened next?
He held out a chicken bone
And then – and then
She said 'I can't eat that!'

◆ EPISODE 4

The witch cannot wait, and decides to eat Hansel. She lights the oven, and asks Gretel to see if it is hot enough. She wants to push Gretel in the oven, but Gretel plays a *trick* on the witch:

What did Gretel think?
I'll push her in the fire
What did Gretel say?
Please can you show me
What happened next?
She crept up to the witch
And then – and then
She pushed her in the fire
Bang!

◆ EPISODE 5: THE HAPPY ENDING

And that was the end of the witch
Hooray!
And Hansel and Gretel went home
Bye Bye
And they lived
Happily ever after
Hooray!

Sleeping Beauty

This story was written for a group of teenagers, one of whom was nearly always asleep due to health reasons. We placed him in the middle of the circle of participants, and although he slept through most of the sessions, he was literally the centre of attention. The final episode, kip rap, was done for him. Most of the episodes refer to famous Hollywood films, and the call and response lines were done 'in character'. This was simply for fun, and participants were invited to suggest characters whose distinctive voices (eg, John Wayne) could be imitated. As an additional entertainment, it is the storyteller who does not know what is going on, and who is continually prompted by the rest of the group. Some of the episodes are based upon mishearing words, as in 'Jack and the Beanstalk'.

◆ EPISODE 1: CHORUS

What's the story?
Sleeping Beauty
Sleeping Blue Knee?
No – Sleeping Beauty
Keeping Beauty?
No – Sleeping Beauty
Keeping Fruity?
No – Sleeping Beauty
Kipping Deeply?
That's close enough.

◆ EPISODE 2

Orson Wells is... the thirteenth auntie

My name is Katchega
Ooooh
And I am very angry
Ooooh
I am the thirteenth auntie
Ooooh
You are going to pay for this
Ooooh
You didn't invite me
So

She will sleep for a hundred years
Get real, Granny!!

◆ EPISODE 3

But Granny puts Sleeping Beauty to sleep (in the style of Robert de Niro in *Taxi Driver*).

Good day, Granny, what's that?
Are you talking to *me*?
Good day, Granny, what's that?
Are *you* talking to *me*?
Good day, Granny, what's that?
Are you talking to me?
Good day, Granny, what's that?
A ticket to Westminster Abbey.
ZZzzzzzzz ...

◆ EPISODE 4: CHORUS

What's going on?
She's bored to snores
She's poured some more
She's bored to snores
She's gored the boar
She's bored to snores
She's floored the door
She's bored to snores
Will you listen!

◆ EPISODE 5: CHORUS

What's going on?
She must wake up
She must make up
She must wake up
She must take up
She must wake up
She must shake up
She must wake up
Will you listen!!

◆ EPISODE 6

Rick the gardener (Humphrey Bogart from *Casablanca*) is a former nightclub owner. He's depressed – and then he finds someone asleep in his garden:

Of all the gardens
Of all the gardens
In all the castles
In all the castles
In all the world
In all the world
And she's asleep in mine
And she's asleep in mine
Here's looking at you kid
[*big sloppy kiss sound*].

◆ EPISODE 7

The prince sorts out the wicked witch (Clint Eastwood as 'Dirty Harry'):

I know what you're thinking punk
I know what you're thinking punk
Has he shot five or six?
Has he shot five or six?
You got to ask yourself one question
You got to ask yourself one question
Do I feel lucky?
Do I feel lucky?
Well do you feel lucky?
Well do you feel lucky?
Punk?
Punk?
Make my day!
Make my day!

◆ **EPISODE 8: FINALE – KIP RAP**

Come on SB what up with you?
Come on SB what up with you?
You fast asleep there's lots to do
You fast asleep there's lots to do
You can chill out, but don't you freeze
You can chill out, but don't you freeze
Hang out with us and shoot the breeze
Hang out with us and shoot the breeze
Wicked!

The Three Little Pigs

In this interactive version of 'The Three Little Pigs', each child has a small box of objects, and is encouraged by a member of staff to hold and manipulate each object at the appropriate time. Each box contains some bits of straw, several sticks tied together (for the roof of sticks), some pieces of brick (for the house of brick), a piece of fake fur for the wolf, and a water sprayer for a member of staff to use when the 'wolf' falls in the cooking pot. Various lines can be recorded on to Big Mack switches or step-by-step communicators to encourage the interactivity. We also consult the school physiotherapist and speech and language therapist so that appropriate movement and communication aims can be included for each child during the activity. This develops storytelling into an interdisciplinary exercise. The narrator speaks the introductory line, and the rest of the story follows in call and response, each line of which (apart from the final section) is 12 beats. The strong repetitive rhythms, combined with the call and response, encourage children to become more engaged in the activity.

◆ EPISODE 1

Once upon a time there were three little pigs. The first pig built a house of straw. The wolf came to the door, and he said:

> Little pig, let me in, little pig, let me in! [mime knocking on the door]
> *No, no, no, by the hair on my chinny chin chin!* [signing 'no, no, no']
> Little pig, let me in, little pig, let me in! [mime knocking on the door]
> *No, no, no, by the hair on my chinny chin chin!* [signing 'no, no, no']
> Then I'll huff and I'll puff, and I'll blow your house down [holding then releasing the straw]
> And he huffed [gasp]; and he puffed [gasp]; and he blew the house down!

[Everyone falls sideways to activate their switch that says 'crash!']

◆ EPISODE 2

The second pig built a house of sticks. The wolf came to the door, and he said:

Little pig, let me in, little pig, let me in! [mime knocking on the door]
No, no, no, by the hair on my chinny chin chin! [signing 'no, no, no']
Little pig, let me in, little pig, let me in! [mime knocking on the door]
No, no, no, by the hair on my chinny chin chin! [signing 'no, no, no']
Then I'll huff and I'll puff, and I'll blow your house down [holding then releasing
    the sticks]
And he huffed [gasp]; and he puffed [gasp]; and he blew the house down!

◆ EPISODE 3

The third pig built a house of bricks. The wolf came to the door, and he said:

Little pig, let me in, little pig, let me in! [mime knocking on the door]
No, no, no, by the hair on my chinny chin chin! [signing 'no, no, no']
Little pig, let me in, little pig, let me in! [mime knocking on the door]
No, no, no, by the hair on my chinny chin chin! [signing 'no, no, no']
Then I'll huff and I'll puff, and I'll blow your house down [holding, and keeping,
    the brick]
And he huffed [gasp]; and he puffed [gasp];
And he huffed [gasp]; and he puffed [gasp];
And he couldn't blow the house down!
Thank goodness! [recorded on all the switches]

◆ EPISODE 4

So the wolf and the pig said to each other:

Now I'll climb down the chimney
I'll catch him in the pot
I'll catch that little piggy
The water's very hot!
Oooohhh!

[Spray everyone with a water sprayer – having carefully considered if this is appropriate for
the people concerned and the venue – ensure it is only clean water.]

Goldilocks

This story was designed for a group of young children with very complex needs, and who needed to have physiotherapy when the timetable said they should be doing literacy. The multidisciplinary team fitted the physiotherapy movements to the story, and so did both. For example, the mock temper tantrum 'Waaah' sounds were done in time to passive leg-stretching exercises.

◆ EPISODE 1

Goldilocks is a naughty girl – she will not get up!

Goldilocks you must get up
I won't get up, I won't get up
Goldilocks it's time for school
I won't get up, I won't get up
Goldilocks you've got to go
I won't get up, I won't get up
Goldilocks you must!
Waaah!

Goldilocks you must get washed
I don't want to, I don't want to
Goldilocks you must get dressed
I don't want to, I don't want to
Goldilocks you must have breakfast
I don't want to, I don't want to
Goldilocks you must!
Waaah!

She goes for a walk in the woods, and finds the house of the bears. They have gone out, so she makes herself at home:

Goldilocks tasted Daddy Bear's porridge
Too hot, too hot
Goldilocks tasted Mummy Bear's porridge
Too cold, too cold
Goldilocks tasted Baby Bear's porridge
Just right, just right
Then she ate the lot
Oooohhhh!

Goldilocks sat in Daddy Bear's chair
Too hard, too hard
Goldilocks sat in Mummy Bear's chair
Too soft, too soft
Goldilocks sat in Baby Bear's chair
Just right, just right
And then she broke it
Oooohhhh!

Goldilocks got into Daddy Bear's bed
Too hard, too hard
Goldilocks got into Mummy Bear's bed
Too soft, too soft
Goldilocks got into Baby Bear's bed
Just right, just right
And then she fell asleep
Oooohhhh!

◆ EPISODE 2

The bears came back. One after another they said:

And who's been eating my porridge?
It's Goldilocks, it's Goldilocks
And who's been eating my porridge?
It's Goldilocks, it's Goldilocks
And who's been eating my porridge?
It's Goldilocks, it's Goldilocks
And it's all gone
Waaah!

And who's been sitting in my chair?
It's Goldilocks, it's Goldilocks
And who's been sitting in my chair?
It's Goldilocks, it's Goldilocks
And who's been sitting in my chair?
It's Goldilocks, it's Goldilocks
And it's broken
Waaah!

And who's been sleeping in my bed?
It's Goldilocks, it's Goldilocks
And who's been sleeping in my bed?
It's Goldilocks, it's Goldilocks
And who's been sleeping in my bed?
It's Goldilocks, it's Goldilocks
And she's still there
Grr!

So Goldilocks ran home and she never went to the woods again.

Little Red Riding Hood

As with 'Hansel and Gretel' this story looks at the difference between appearance and reality. It has been done with children as young as one year old with their carers.

◆ EPISODE 1: GRANNY TO GO

Little Red Riding Hood has gone to see her Granny, but the Wolf has got there first. He has a dialogue with the group – who are all Grannies – as follows:

I knock on the door
[*knock four times*]
She says, 'Who's there?'
Who's there, who's there?
Red Riding Hood
Red Riding Hood
And I go IN
Aarrgghh!

Activity
The Wolf prowls around the inside of the circle. He is pretending *to be Red Hiding Hood. At the beginning of the last line, the Wolf* points *to a victim, approaches them, and then 'gets' them by covering them with a small piece of red cloth. Everyone screams!*

◆ EPISODE 2: WHAT BIG EYES YOU'VE GOT!

Red Riding Hood gets to her Granny's house and knocks at the door. That is Granny ... isn't it?

O Granny what big EYES you've got
All the better to SEE you with
O Granny what big EARS you've got
All the better to HEAR you with
O Granny what big TEETH you've got
All the better to EAT you with!
Aarrgghh!

Activity
On the final line the Wolf leaps up and tries to catch one of the Red Riding Hoods, while they try to escape by returning to their places. The Red Riding Hood victim could be covered by the cloak and then uncovered so that she can 'show herself'.

◆ **EPISODE 3: CATCHING THE WOLF**

The hunters are chasing the Wolf. Will they catch him?

Now can you catch
Now can you catch
The Big Bad Wolf?
The Big Bad Wolf?
It's [name]'s turn
It's [name]'s turn
And GO!

Activity
The Wolf, in the middle, starts a dialogue with the group to choose the hunter. The Wolf is choosing a 'hunter' by pointing around the circle at everyone in turn. The person who is chosen moves towards the Wolf and tries to touch him, before the Wolf can escape.

Snow White – Drifted

This tongue-in-cheek version of 'Snow White' was made for a group of teenagers: so the mirror speaks like Ali G and has a bad memory; Snow White is a picky eater, and the raspberry is spiked with something illegal, making Snow White wake up with a hangover.

◆ EPISODE 1

The wicked queen talks to her mirror. But the mirror has amnesia:

> Mirror mirror on the wall
> *Mirror mirror on the wall*
> Who is the fairest of them all?
> *Who's the fairest of them all?*
> It's George Bush?
> *Oh no it isn't*
> It's the Queen?
> *Oh no it isn't*
> It's Elton John?
> *Oh no it isn't*
> So you tell me
> *It's Snow White – innit!*

Activity
Everyone calls out the beginning, as well as the end, of this activity. Make up names for the forgetful mirror to call out. The final line can be done Ali G-style, with suitable gestures.

◆ EPISODE 2

In the forest, Snow White meets the seven couch potatoes, who make her an offer:

> You do the shopping
> *You do the shopping*
> You cook the dinner
> *You cook the dinner*
> You do the washing up
> *You do the washing up*

You do the ironing
You do the ironing
You walk the dog
You walk the dog
We don't do housework
We don't do housework
We're couch potatoes
We're couch potatoes
Get a life!

Activity

Snow White can wear a white glittery blanket and be in the middle of the circle. Everyone points at her, or looks at her, throughout the exchange. Everyone calls out the final line, which is her response to the seven dwarves.

◆ EPISODE 3

The wicked queen finds Snow White and offers her an apple, but Snow White eats only red food:

Would you like an apple?
Yuk! Oh no!
Would you like a banana?
Yuk! Oh no!
Would you like some grapes?
Yuk! Oh no!
Would you like a raspberry?
Oh, yes please!
[Everyone blows a raspberry]

Activity

The response ('Yuk! Oh no!') can be on the single switches. Snow White is in the middle of the circle, and is the recipient of the raspberry!

◆ EPISODE 4

Snow White eats the poisoned raspberry. The wicked queen shouts:

Red as blood
Red as blood
White as snow
White as snow

Black as ebony
Black as ebony
Snow White!
Snow White!
Good night!
Good night!
[*Manic laugh*]

Activity

Everyone is in a circle. A glittery blanket is held upright and waved throughout the exchange. On the line 'Good Night!', someone is covered up as everyone does a mad laugh in the style of the Wicked Witch of the West from The Wizard of Oz.

◆ EPISODE 5

Snow White falls asleep, possibly because of lack of food:

Doze and slumber
Doze and slumber
Snooze and kip
Snooze and kip
Drowsy
Drowsy
Sleepy
Sleepy
Snow White
Snow White
Sleep tight
Sleep tight
Oi! You! Wake up!

Activity

Snow White is in the middle of the circle. Participants in the circle gently wave a parachute up and down throughout the exchange, which is very slow and quiet. On the final line it is held up as everyone shouts, 'Oi! You! Wake up!' at Snow White (who can have a switch with a snore recorded on it).

◆ **EPISODE 6**

Snow White wakes up. What was in that raspberry?

Hello boys
Hello boys
Where's the party?
Where's the party?
Let's have fun
Let's have fun
Where's my drink?
Where's my drink?
I used to be Snow White
I used to be Snow White
But I drifted
But I drifted
Ha ha ha
Hooray!

Activity
These lines are done with everyone swaying from side to side and speaking in a 'morning after the night before' style. The phrase 'I used to be Snow White, but I drifted' has been attributed to Mae West.

Chapter 2

Stories from Around the World

Stories from Around the World

The first three of the stories in this chapter were made by the staff of William C Harvey School (North London) during a storytelling course. Workshop participants divided themselves into groups of four or five and were invited to rework a poem or story of their choice into an interactive version. Groups who had more than one ethnic background were encouraged to suggest a poem or story from their non-English cultures. At the end of the afternoon each group presented its story to the others. The school staff have kindly agreed for these examples to be published and used by anyone. It is recommended that, if posible, you have access to someone from the specific culture to offer advice on pronunciation. The third story is not derived from an original source, but was made up on the day.

Yorba Song – from Nigeria (Ibo language)

Stand in a circle singing or chanting the song. Repeat two or three times.
End by dancing back to your seats.

Iwe Kiko
Iwe Kiko
Laisi Koko
Laisi Koko
Ati ada
Ati ada
Koi pe o
Koi pe o

This means 'education without farming is incomplete'!

Anansi Story – Ghanaian legend

A group of creatures flew over the sea
On their way to a tea party
A tea party, a tea party
With jelly and ice cream
Um! That's for me!
Anansi the spider called, 'Wait for me'
Wait for me
'I want to come to your tea party'
Your tea party. Ooooh!
He had no wings so the others said:
'Come fix some feathers to your eight hairy legs'
Eight hairy legs, Eight hairy legs
Come fix some feathers to your eight hairy legs.

They got to the party and Anansi said:
'Let's change our names to these instead'
They all chose names and Anansi said:
'They're good names and mine is ...'
All-of-you
They're good names and mine is
All-of-you. Ooooh!

The hostess arrived with her tray of food
'Please help yourself, it's for all of you'
Please help yourself, it's for all of you
'If 'All-of-you' is my new name ...'
The spider took the food and made his claim
He made his claim, he made his claim
Anansi the spider, he made his claim
Ooooh!

The rest of them did not agree
Did not agree, did not agree
They plucked their feathers from Anansi
They plucked their feathers from Anansi.

They left him there at the tea party
At the tea party, at the tea party
And flew back home o'er the big wide sea
The big wide sea, the big wide sea. Ooooh!

The First Kiss – a story in English and Arabic

Crazy	No
Crazy	*No*
Magnuna	La-ahh
Magnuna	*La-ahh*
Shut up	Give me a kiss
Shut up	*Give me a kiss*
Escottee	Idinee busa
Escottee	*Idinee busa*
Sorry	Yes
Sorry	*Yes*
Malesh	Naum
Malesh	*Naum*
Give me a kiss	Kiss
Give me a kiss	*Kiss*
Idinee busa	Busa
Idinee busa	*Busa*

Seruhsee – a story from Guyana

This story is from BJ Martin, who presented the story at a workshop in Lewisham (south London) and who described it as follows:

The poem is based on a Guyanese folk-song. It tells the story of a mother and her daughter, and the daughter's introduction to the latest herbal tea, Seruhsee. This is a herbal tea used for stomach ailments, diabetes, and joint pains. Unfortunately, Helena does not recognise the correct herbs to infuse and picks the wrong one! Her mother soon puts her right!

Helena an' shi mumma goh ah grung
What?
Helena an' shi mumma goh a grung
Ohhhhhh!
Helena start cry fih shi belly
What?
Helena start cry fih shi belly
Ahhhhhh!
Go home Helena
Go home Helena
Go bwoil Seruhsee fih yuh belly
Go bwoil Seruhsee fih yuh belly.

Di mumma shi dig an' shi plant
What?
Di mumma shi dig an' shi plant
Ohhhhhh!
But shi min' dis ah run pon Helena
What?
Shi min' dis ah run pon Helena
Ahhhhhh!
Shi tek up shi bag
Shi basket an' shi cutlass
An' goh home fih goh look fih Helena
An' goh home fih goh look fih Helena.

Di mumma ketch home ah di yard
Where?
Di mumma ketch home ah di yard
Oh the house!
Shi see di bu'n pot pon di fire
What?
Shi see di bu'n pot pon di fire
Pon di fire?
Shi tek piece o' stick
An' shi stir an' shi stir
An' di Night Sage ah cum by di bungle
An' di Night Sage ah cum by di bungle.

Gal ah wah dis yuh bwoil fih yuh belly?
What?
Gal ah wah dis yuh bwoil fih yuh belly?
Herb Tea!
Gal ah payson yuh bwoil fih yuh belly?
What?
Gal ah payson yuh bwoil fih yuh belly?
Seruhsee!
Fro' yuh barn cum a worl'
Yuh nuh know Seruhsee
Gal yuh foolish, yuh foolish, yuh foolish
Gal yuh foolish, yuh foolish, yuh foolish!

Di mumma shi tek some Seruhsee
Herb Tea!
Di mumma shi tek some Seruhsee
Seruhsee!
Shi bwoil it an' gih it to Helena
Go Helena!
Yes, shi bwoil it an' gi it to Helena
Drink Helena!
Helena shi drink it
An' shi sleep, an' shi sleep
An' she wake up widout pain a' belly
An' shi wake up widout pain a' belly.

Look good pon Seruhsee, Helena
Helena
Look good pon Seruhsee Helena
Look good!
Di leaf, an di vine, an di berry
What?
Di leaf, an di vine, an di berry
Ahhhhhh!
Come know Seruhsee
An' 'member Seruhsee
Cos ah it cure yuh bad pain a' belly
Cos ah it cure yuh bad pain a' belly
Wicked!

Dis is Grama Alfabet – a story from Jamaica

'A'   is for Ackee
         qualifies with fish

'B'   is for Bami
         yami yami

'C'   is for Callaloo
         Oo ... Makes you poo! But it gud fi u

'D'   is for Dumpling
         Lard ... It tie up yu tripe

'E'   is for Elephan
         Lard, wat a brute dem big

'F'   is for Fri Fish
         wat a taysti dish

'G'   is for Guava
         remine me av mi madda (mother)

'H'   is for Heaven
         Lard... a de mi grannie gan!

'I'   is a Pronon
         wich una al mus lerne

'J'   is for Jackass
         plentie go tu skool

'K'   is for Kingston
         de Kapital av Jamdone

'L'   is for Layer (lawyer)
           dem tel tu moch ly

'M'   is for Money
           if u ave it... u wol seil

'N'   is for Nancie
           de spyda man

'O'   fava Q
           but it likkle bit stout

'P'   is for Punch
           if u drink tu moch – u fart

'Q'   is for Queen
           an dat is me

'R'   is for Rom + Riddim (music)
           ton di bes man foole

'S'   is for Suga
           swite laik me

'T'   is for Tongue
            onu chat tu much

'U'   is You
           an u – an u – an u

'V'   is for Veranda
           sit outside to cool

'W'   is for Water
           u need plenti in da sun

'X', 'Y', 'Z'   Hime fir bed.

dat dun.

Dr Who – a story from another galaxy

Look at the Box!
What box?
That box there
What box where?
That box there
It's the Tardis
oh yeah!

Shall we go in?
Yes we'll go in
Shall we go in?
Yes we'll go in
Who's going in?
[name] going in
Who's going in?
[name] going in.

Who's in the box?
He's in the box
Who, who?
I'm Doctor Who
Who, who?
I'm Doctor Who

We're all in the box
We're all in the box
Close the door
Close the door
Countdown commencing
Countdown commencing
Off with a roar
Off with a roar
5, 4, 3, 2, 1 [everyone stamps feet, etc, getting louder and louder]

WHOOOSH!

Everyone calls out *Dr Who* theme music, which of course goes as follows:

dum di dum dum di dum, dum di dum dum dum
dum di dum dum di dum, dum di dum dum dum
dum di dum dum di dum, dum di dum dum dum
dum di dum dum di dum, dum di dum dum dum
Woo-oooooooooooooooooooooooooooooh!

Jonah – a Bible story in Cockney rhyming slang

The Bible in Cockney is a retelling of some famous Bible stories in Cockney rhyming slang, by Mike Coles (2001). Inspired by this book, the following story was written for a school where most of the staff and children are of Cockney origin, and the original script was gradually changed by the staff group to reflect phrases that were currently in use locally. Rhyming slang is based on a rhyme, the second part of which is often dropped, leaving the first part as the 'rhyming slang' for the original word. So, the phrase 'dog and bone' means 'phone', but often the single word 'dog' will be used. 'Loaf of bread' is rhyming slang for 'head', but usually the 'loaf' is used by itself. The rhyming slang used in this story is explained as each phrase occurs.

◆ EPISODE 1

God tells Jonah to go to Nineveh, but Jonah says:

> Nineveh – no way!
> I'm gonna leg it!
> I'm off to Spain
> On board a nanny [nanny = nanny goat = boat]
> 'E won't find me there!
> God was watching
> God sent a strong wind
> Blowing on the coffee [coffee = coffee and tea = sea]
> The nanny might sink!
> *Would you Adam and Eve it!* [Adam and Eve it = believe it]

◆ EPISODE 2

The sailors speak to Jonah:

> What's your game then?
> Where d'you come from?
> I'm on the hot cross bun from 'im [on the hot cross bun = on the run]
> Throw me in the coffee
> This all my fault

So they picked 'im up
Chucked 'im in the coffee
The storm calmed dahn
Would you Adam and Eve it!

◆ EPISODE 3

Jonah is thrown into the sea:

Jonah floated in the coffee
A great big Lillian Gish [Lillian Gish = fish]
Swallowed 'im right up
From inside the Lillian
Jonah said: 'O God
I'm in a two-and-eight [in a two-and-eight = in a state, or in other words 'a right mess']
Choking in the fisherman's [fisherman's = fisherman's daughter = water]
Covered by the coffee
Seaweed round me loaf [loaf = loaf of bread = head]
Thought I was brown bread [brown bread = dead]
I'll do what you want'
The Lillian
Spat 'im out
Would you Adam and Eve it!

◆ EPISODE 4

So Jonah went to Nineveh and said to the people:

Listen up, you lot!
Sort yourselves out
Or Nineveh will be destroyed
They gave up their dodgy ways
They said sorry
God was well 'appy
God forgave 'em all
Would you Adam and Eve it!

David and Goliath – a Bible story in Cockney rhyming slang

◆ EPISODE 1

The Philistines and the Israelites are at war:

Israelites over 'ere
Philistines over there
Both armies on a jack [Jack and Jill = hill]
Some geezer called Goliath [geezer = person]
Says 'I'm a Philistine
You're pathetic
Find someone
To 'ave it out with me
If you think you're 'ard enough
Come and get it if you think you're 'ard enough!'

◆ EPISODE 2

So David said to King Saul:

With respect, Guv
We're the army of God, right?
And this Goliath geezer
Needs a good kicking
All I need is a sling
And me shepherd's stick
And five stones
'E's a diamond geezer! [roughly translated as 'he's a very good man']

◆ EPISODE 3

Goliath came out and saw David:

> Is that the best you got?
> I'll chop you to bits
> Feed you to the Richards [Richard the Third = birds]
> David got a stone
> Put it in 'is sling
> Swung it round and round
> Slung it at Goliath
> Got 'im in the 'ed
> *Sorted!*

The Magic Pudding – a story from Australia

Oh who would be a puddin'
A puddin' in a pot
A puddin' which is stood in
A fire which is hot
O sad indeed the lot
Of puddin's in a pot

I wouldn't be a puddin'
If I could be a bird
If I could be a wooden
Doll, I wouldn't say a word
Yes, I have often heard
It's grand to be a bird

But since I am a puddin'
A puddin' in a pot
I hope you get the stomach-ache
For eatin' me a lot
I hope you get it hot
You puddin' eatin' lot!

Eat away, chew away
Munch and bolt and guzzle
Never leave the table
Til you're full up to the muzzle
Wurgh!

Bir Atallah – a story from Egypt

بير عطا لله

Nevin Gouda has said that when she was a child growing up in Egypt, her grandmother would tell her the story of 'The Well of Truth'. Nevin's grandmother had learned the story from her grandmother, who in turn had heard it from hers, and so on back through the generations. We adapted it and included some Arabic phrases to give participants the opportunity to play with the language. As far as we know, this is the first time the story has ever been produced in a written format.

◆ EPISODE 1

Once upon a time there was an old woman who lived with her animal friends: a cow, a dog, a horse, a rooster, a sheep and a cat. One day, the woman baked a pie. She put it on the table and went outside:

> But no-one saw
> That cat creep in
> That greedy cat
> That naughty cat
> Ate up all the pie
> لا لا لا
> *Lair, lair, lair!* [*no! no! no!*]

◆ EPISODE 2

So:

Who ate that pie?
> 'Mosh Ana,' said the cow
> 'Mosh Ana,' said the dog
> 'Mosh Ana,' said the horse
> 'Mosh Ana,' said the rooster
> 'Mosh Ana,' said the sheep
> 'Mosh Ana,' said the cat
> مش أنا
> *Mosh Ana!* [*not me!*]

◆ **EPISODE 3**

What next?

> Now we must go
> To Atallah
> Bir Atallah
> Well of Truth
> يالا يالا يالا
> *Yalla! Yalla! Yalla!* [*Let's go!*]

Activity
The first four lines are spoken quietly and slowly, before the last line is called out fast and loud as everyone stamps their feet up and down as they 'run' to the well.

◆ **EPISODE 4**

The animals go to the well. The cow says:

> 'I did not tell a lie
> I did not eat that pie
> I'll jump across the well'

> هيلا هوبا

> *Hayla!*
> *Hoppa!*
> *Oi, Oi, Oi!*
> [repeat for dog, horse, rooster, sheep until the last verse]

The cat says:

> 'I d-d-did not tell a lie
> I d-d-did not eat that pie'
> And falls down the well!
> *Splat!*

Activity
The animals are cheered as they jump across the Well of Truth – except the cat, who pays the price for telling a fib!

◆ **EPISODE 5**

Let's help the cat out of the well:

[name] Anajdah النجدة [help me]
[name] Anajdah النجدة
Ready, steady
Go!
Hooray!

Activity
A 4 metre piece of lycra (or other cloth) is stretched between the participants, as the 'well' on which a toy cat is placed. The cloth is moved up and down and, on 'Go!', the cat is 'pulled' out of the well (in fact it usually bounces off the ceiling).

Chapter 3
Shakespeare

Shakespeare

Each of the following workshops has been performed on the stage of Shakespeare's Globe Theatre. Greenwich and Lewisham are both very close to the theatre, and this made it quite easy for the schools to get there and back in a morning. The Globe education staff continue to be extremely supportive in the development of these workshops. The theatre is an authentic reconstruction of the original Globe Theatre of 1599 and has a 14 metre (40 foot) wooden stage that provides a wonderful resonance for the poetry workshops.

Although the storyline of each play is followed, the emphasis of the activities is not so much the narrative as the power of Shakespearian poetry. For this reason each workshop uses extracts of original text, which are performed in 'call and response', with everyone calling out the final line together. As with the other stories, these activities have the format of a communication game that aims to engage everyone. In every episode of these workshops, except where indicated otherwise by response lines in italics, each call line is identical to each response line.

Shakespeare's monumental and enduring influence on English language and culture has been described by Bernard Levin in one long and enthusiastic sentence:

> If you cannot understand my argument, and declare 'It's Greek to me', you are quoting Shakespeare; if you claim to be more sinned against than sinning, you are quoting Shakespeare; if you recall your salad days, you are quoting Shakespeare; if you act more in sorrow than in anger, if your wish is father to the thought, if your property has vanished into thin air, you are quoting Shakespeare; if you have ever refused to budge an inch or suffered from green-eyed jealousy, if you have played fast and loose, if you have been tongue-tied, a tower of strength, hoodwinked or in a pickle, if you have knitted your brows, made a virtue of necessity, insisted on fair play, slept not one wink, stood on ceremony, danced attendance (on your lord and master), laughed yourself into stitches, had short shrift, cold comfort or too much of a good thing, if you have seen better days or lived in a fool's paradise – why, be that as it may, the more fool you, for it is a foregone conclusion that you are (as good luck would have it) quoting Shakespeare; if you think it is early days and clear out bag and baggage, if you think it is high time and that is the long and short of it, if you believe that the game is up and that truth will out even if it involves your own flesh and blood, if you lie low till the crack of doom because you suspect foul play, if you have your teeth set on edge (at one fell swoop) without rhyme or reason, then – to give the devil his due – if the truth were known (for surely you have a tongue in your head), you are quoting Shakespeare; even if you bid me good riddance and send me packing, if you wish I was dead as a doornail, if you think I am an eyesore, a laughing stock, the devil incarnate, a stony-hearted villain, bloody-minded or a blinking idiot, then – by Jove! O Lord! Tut, tut! for goodness sake! what the dickens! but me no buts – it is all one to me, for you are quoting Shakespeare. (Levin, 1983, pp167–8).

A Midsummer Night's Dream

◆ EPISODE 1: OBERON

Oberon, the king of the fairies, is having an argument with his queen, Titania. He decides to teach her a lesson, and puts a magic herb on her eyes as she sleeps. She will fall in love with whatever she sees first when waking up – Bottom, with the head of a donkey. Titania is snoring ...

> *Zzzzzzzzzzzzzz...*
> What thou seest when thou dost wake
> Do it for thy true-love take
> When thou wakest, it is thy dear
> Wake when some vile thing is near
> *Eee – Eee – Eee – Eee orr!*
> I pray thee, gentle mortal, sing again
> *Eee orr! Eee orr! Eee orr!*

Activity

One person (or two or three) is in the middle of the circle as Titania. The lines are spoken in call and response, after the exchange is initiated by Titania, with the snoring sound recorded on the switch. The first 'Eee orr' is done rather like a sneeze ('Eee Eee Eee Eee orr!' = 'Aah Aah Aah Choo!'), to provide an exaggerated anticipation. The donkey sounds can then be repeated twice more – and even louder – in reply to Titania's words on waking up.

◆ EPISODE 2: HERMIA TO HELENA

Helena and Hermia are lost in the woods and are very cross with each other. In the play, Helena is often played by someone tall and Hermia by someone short, hence the 'painted maypole' and 'dwarf' insults in the next two extracts.

> You puppet, you!
> Painted maypole!
> How low am I?
> Not yet so low
> But that my nails
> Can reach into
> Thine eyes!
> *Aaarrgghh!*

Activity

This activity is initiated by Helena's words 'You puppet you!', prerecorded on the switch. Hermia's lines are spoken with simulated anger, starting quietly and getting louder each line, until the 'Aarrgghh' is screamed out with everyone stamping their feet and waving their arms in a simulated temper tantrum. If Helena's words are repeated by the switch user throughout the exchange, it contributes to the effect of two people having a noisy argument. One or more participants can be 'Helena' in the middle of the circle, to provide a focal point for Hermia's invective.

◆ EPISODE 3: HELENA AND LYSANDER, TO HERMIA

Helena and Lysander take their turn at insulting Hermia.

> *Oooohhhh!*
> When she's angry
> She is keen and shrewd
> Though she be but little
> She is fierce
> Get you gone you dwarf
> You minimus
> You bead
> You acorn
> *Oooohhhh!*

Activity

The 'Oooohhhh!' on a switch starts this exchange, which we do in a pantomime 'ooh get you' style (think of Julian Clary) to provide a contrast to the previous activity. The activity finishes with everyone putting their hands on their hips and calling out a very exaggerated 'Oooohhhh!'. Participants might want to suggest other characters whose style can be imitated – Clint Eastwood ('make my day') or Jimmy Cagney ('you dirty rat!'). The full version of Lysander's 'minimus' insult is the wonderfully silly 'you minimus of hindering knotgrass!', which can be used as an alternative to 'you bead, you acorn'. As the participants say 'knotgrass!', they can kick the stage floor as if stumbling or stepping on something unpleasant, and then give a loud 'Oooohhhh!'.

◆ EPISODE 4: BOTTOM

After his midsummer night's dream, Bottom wakes up and announces: 'I will get Peter Quince to write a ballad of this dream: it shall be called Bottom's Dream, because it hath no bottom'. But he just cannot get the words right.

Eee orr
I have had a dream
Methought I was –
Methought I had –
The eye of man
Hath not heard
The ear of man
Hath not seen
What my dream was
Man is but an ass
Eee orr!

Activity

The 'Eee orr' that dominates this exchange is heavily ironic: an 'Eee orr' that means something like 'stu–pid'. Anyone who has ever seen John Cleese and others playing the very gormless Mr and Mrs Gumby (knotted handkerchief on head, rolling eyes, trousers rolled up, arms held out like penguin flippers, and calling out 'Dhhrrr!') may have a role model.

◆ EPISODE 5: PYRAMUS AND THISBE

'This is the silliest stuff that ever I heard.' So says one of the characters about the play 'Pyramus and Thisbe' presented by Bottom and his friends to the nobles at court. It ends with Pyramus, believing Thisbe to be dead, stabbing himself; Thisbe then appears, sees Pyramus dead, and duly stabs herself.

Oooohhhh
O Fates, come, come!
Cut thread and thrum
Quail and crush,
Conclude and quell!
And farewell friends
Thus Thisbe ends
Adieu
Adieu
Byeeee!

Activity

There is a chance for some real over-the-top acting, with the words being accompanied by grand sweeping gestures. A prerecorded melodramatic groan – 'Oooohhhh' – on a switch initiates the activity, and can then be repeated throughout, to accentuate the comedy of the awful acting. A large glittery blanket (the wall through which Pyramus and Thisbe have been talking) is held up by one or two people so that everyone can see it. It is gradually lowered over someone as the 'adieus' are called out, and then thrown over them as everyone suddenly shouts 'Byeeee!'

◆ EPISODE 6: 'LET THE AUDIENCE LOOK TO THEIR EYES'

So says Bottom, convinced that their play 'Pyramus and Thisbe' will move the audience to tears. *A Midsummer Night's Dream* is full of references to eyes and the imagery of vision. Helena says 'Love looks not with the eyes but with the mind', and that Demetrius is 'doting on Hermia's eyes' – an indication that this might not be true love. All the mistakes follow from magic potions to the eyes. Here is a brief selection of poetic images about eyes and vision from the play. Lines five and six are spoken by Hermia as the two couples wake up in the woods the next morning, dazed and confused. The final two lines are Oberon's, as he releases Titania from the magic spell of her love for the donkey-headed Bottom.

> *Sssshhhh*
> Upon thy eyes I throw
> All the power this charm doth owe
> I see these things with parted eye
> When every thing seems double
> I will her charmed eye release
> And all things shall be peace
> *Sssshhhh*

Activity
These lines are spoken quietly, initiated by the switch user's 'Sssshhhh', while a parachute is gently raised and lowered over all participants. As the final long 'Sssshhhh' is spoken, the parachute is released and covers everyone, and is followed by as long a silence as possible. This is a calm and quiet activity to end the workshop.

Othello

This workshop is an exploration of *Othello* with which we use three languages: English and phrases from Arabic and BSL. There are six sections: Episodes 1, 3 and 5 are words spoken by Iago (who makes Othello believe that his wife is unfaithful, and encourages him to murder her) and Episodes 2, 4 and 6 are spoken by Othello (who believes Iago's words, murders his wife, then realises what a terrible mistake he has made and kills himself). Shakespeare entitled the play 'The Tragedy of Othello, The Moor of Venice' – as a Moor, Othello's first language would have been Arabic. In these activities, English and Arabic are used to indicate the powerful emotions that arise from Iago's destruction of Othello and Desdemona. The text is arranged so that the Arabic script (which reads from right to left) appears in the middle of the page, the English translation is to the right of the page, and the phonetic equivalent of the Arabic word is to the left of the page. Anyone who wants to use this material is advised to do so in consultation with someone who speaks Arabic as a first language. Many thanks to BJ Martin, who provided us with the tuition in BSL to enable phrases from BSL to be used with the English and Arabic script.

◆ **EPISODE 1: LOVE AND HATE**

Iago has a plan to destroy Othello and Desdemona:

> I hate the Moor
> Divinity of hell!
> Out of her own goodness
> I'll make the net
> That shall enmesh them all
> Hayem wa و هيام love and
> *Karaheya* كراهية *hate*

◆ **EPISODE 2: LOVE AND WITCHCRAFT**

Othello explains how he and Desdemona fell in love:

She loved me
For the dangers I had passed
And I loved her
That she did pity them
This only is the witchcraft

| Hayem wa | هيام و | love and |
| *Sehr* | سحر | *witchcraft* |

◆ **EPISODE 3: LOVE AND JEALOUSY**

Iago warns Othello about jealousy:

O beware, my lord, of jealousy
It is the green-eyed monster
Which doth mock
The meat it feeds on

| Hayem wa | هيام و | love and |
| *Hasad* | حسد | *jealousy* |

◆ **EPISODE 4: LOVE AND VENGEANCE**

Othello believes Iago's lies and swears he will be revenged:

All my fond love
Thus do I blow to heaven

Intaha	إنتهى	'Tis gone
Enhud	إنهض	arise
Ya intiquam	يا إنتقام	
Ya aswad	يا أسود	black vengeance!
Hayem wa	هيام و	love and
Intiquam	إنتقام	*vengeance*

◆ EPISODE 5: LOVE AND DEATH

Iago tells Othello how to kill Desdemona:

Do it not with poison
Strangle her in her bed
Even the bed
She hath contaminated
Hayem wa   هيام و   love and
Maowt   موت   *death*

◆ EPISODE 6: THE END

Othello murders Desdemona, realises he has made a terrible mistake, and then kills himself:

Speak of me as I am
Of one that loved not wisely
But too well
But, being wrought,
Perplex'd in the extreme
Hudoo wa   هدوء و   calm and
Salem   سلام   *peace*

Macbeth

In this workshop, extracts from Holinshed's *Chronicle* – first published in 1577 and the historical basis for Shakespeare's play – are used to provide the prose introduction to the storyline of each activity.

◆ EPISODE 1: ALL HAIL!

suddenlie in the midst of a laund, there met them three women in strange and wild apparell, resembling creatures of elder world, whome when they attentiuelie beheld, wondering much at the sight, the first of them spake and said 'All haile, Makbeth, thane of Glammis!'... The second of them said: 'Haile, Makbeth, thane of Cawdor!' But the third said 'All haile, Makbeth, that heerafter shalt be king of Scotland!'

(Nicoll, J & Nicoll, A [eds], 1927)

1st: When shall we three meet again?
      In thunder, lightning or in rain?

2nd: When the hurly-burly's done,
      When the battle's lost, and won.

3rd: That will be ere the set of sun.

1st: Where the place?

2nd: Upon the heath.

3rd: There to meet with Macbeth.

All: Fair is foul and foul is fair
      Hover through the fog and filthy air.
      All hail Macbeth that shall be king hereafter!

Activity
These opening words of the play, and the final line of the witches' prophetic greeting to Macbeth in Act 1, scene 3, are recited in a low whisper, and then everyone points to a Macbeth, placed in the middle of the circle, on the final line. Try varying the emotional register of the words, for example saying them angrily, sadly or ironically.

◆ EPISODE 2: AN UNQUIET MIND

& speedilie going about the murther, they enter the chamber (in which the king laie) a little before cocks crow, where they secretlie cut his throte as he lay sleeping, without any buskling at all... but yet to himselfe he seemed most vnhappie, as he that could not but still liue in continuall feare, lest his wicked practise concerning the death of Malcome Duffe should come to light and knowledge of the world. For so commeth it to passe, that such as are pricked in conscience for anie secret offense committed, haue euer an vnquiet mind.   (Nicoll, J & Nicoll, A [eds], 1927)

Macbeth shall sleep no more
Macbeth does murder sleep
Hear not my steps
Which way they walk
I go and it is done
Hear – it – not
Murder most foul!

Activity
For this activity, the murder of Duncan, a volunteer Macbeth holds a plastic retractable dagger and slowly approaches the chosen victim. On the words 'hear – it – not' Duncan is stabbed with the dagger, and everyone calls out the final line of 'Murder most foul!'

◆ EPISODE 3: THIRST AFTER BLOOD

At length he found such sweetnesse by putting his nobles to death, that his earnest thirst after blood in this behalfe might in no wise be satisfied.
                                    (Nicoll, J & Nicoll, A [eds], 1927)

It will have blood they say
Blood will have blood
I am in blood
Stepped in so far
It will have blood they say
You

Activity
For this activity we used a small piece of red glittery material as Banquo's blood. Macbeth moves around the circle of participants and then, on the final line of 'you', covers Banquo. Try saying the words in different ways: angry, sad, resigned, bitter, and so on.

◆ EPISODE 4: THE WEIRD SISTERS

But afterwards the common opinion was, that these women were either the weird sisters, that is (as ye would say) the goddesses of destinie, or else some nymphs or feiries, indued with knowledge or prophesie by their necromanticall science, bicause euerie thing came to passe as they had spoken.
                                    (Nicoll, J & Nicoll, A [eds], 1927)

Lines from Act IV, scene i, are chanted in call and response:

Double, double toil and trouble
Fire burn and cauldron bubble.
Fillet of a fenny snake,
In the cauldron boil and bake:
Eye of newt and toe of frog,
Wool of bat, and tongue of dog,
Adder's fork, and blind-worm's sting,
Lizard's leg, and howlet's wing,
For a charm of powerful trouble,
Like a hell-broth, boil and bubble.
Double, double toil and trouble,
Fire burn and cauldron bubble.

Activity
There was very little activity to accompany this powerful piece of text. Everyone remained still and stirred an imaginary pot while the words were chanted, either whispered or shouted, and sometimes sad or rejoicing.

◆ EPISODE 5: THE END

It is true, Makbeth, and now shall thine insatiable crueltie haue an end, for I am euen he that thy wizzards haue told thee of... therewithall he stept vnto him, and slue him in the place. Then cutting his head head from his shoulders, he set it vpon a pole, and brought it vnto Malcome.   (Nicoll, J & Nicoll, A [eds], 1927)

Hell hound!
I will not yield
Villain!
I will not yield
Coward!
I will not yield
Monster!
I will not yield
Tyrant!
I will not yield
Behold the cursed head!
Hooray!

Activity
The acting out of Macduff's insults to Macbeth in Act V, scene viii, and of Macbeth's refusal to yield, started quite loud and then became even louder, ending with a cheer as they lift an imaginary head of Macbeth for everyone to see.

The Tempest

◆ **EPISODE 1: CALIBAN TO PROSPERO**

Caliban, a monster, is the slave of Prospero, who lives on an enchanted island with his daughter, Miranda. Caliban and Prospero hate each other and nearly all of their exchanges are curses and insults. This is Caliban, enraged, cursing both Prospero and Miranda:

Aarrgghh!!
You taught me language
And my profit on't
Is I know how to curse
A south-west blow on ye
And blister you all o'er!
All the charms of Sycorax
Toads, beetles, bats
Light on you!
The red plague rid you
For learning me your language!
Aarrgghh!!

Activity
An angry roar recorded on the switches initiates the activity. The first three lines of this call and response sequence are spoken at average volume, and the rest is shouted, roared and bellowed as loudly as possible. After the final line, participants give a very loud roar of rage and stamp their feet loudly on the stage. A real temper tantrum!

◆ **EPISODE 2: PROSPERO TO CALIBAN**

Prospero answers Caliban's cursing with threats and curses of his own:

[A roar, starting softly and getting very loud]
For this, be sure,
To-night thou shalt have cramps
Thou shalt be pinch'd
As thick as honeycomb
I'll rack thee with old cramps
Fill all thy bones with aches
Make thee roar
[A roar, starting softly and getting very loud]

Activity
These words are spoken in a soft but threatening manner. They are begun and concluded by a roar that begins quietly and builds up to a very loud volume before suddenly stopping, providing a strong contrast between sound and silence.

◆ EPISODE 3: ARIEL TO FERDINAND

Ariel is a spirit controlled by Prospero, who has by magic created a tempest that has caused a shipwreck. Ferdinand, who thinks he may be the only survivor, hears the magical song of Ariel, who seems to be telling him that his father has been drowned.

> [Sound of a bell]
> Full fathom five thy father lies;
> Of his bones are coral made;
> Those are pearls that were his eyes:
> Nothing of him that doth fade,
> But doth suffer a sea-change
> Into something rich and strange
> Sea-nymphs hourly ring his bell
> [Sound of a bell]
> Hark!
> [Sound of a bell]
> Now I hear them
> [Sound of a bell]

Activity
In contrast to the previous activity, this is calm and quiet, beginning and ending with the chiming of pre-recorded, hand-held bells.

◆ EPISODE 4: CALIBAN TO TRINCULO AND STEPHANO

Trinculo, Stephano and Caliban all get drunk together, and Caliban sings that he will no longer serve Prospero:

> [sound of a drunken hiccup!]
> No more dams
> I'll make for fish
> Nor fetch in firing

At requiring
Nor scrape trencher,
Nor wash dish:
'Ban
'Ban
Cacaliban'
Hooray!

Activity
The activity is initiated by loud drunken 'hic!' recorded on all switches. The participants sound a loud and boisterous chant with drums and tambours, and with the penultimate lines ('Ban, 'Ban, Cacaliban') followed by a very loud drunken cheer. They can also sway from side to side.

Language in *The Tempest*
The vocabulary and imagery of the sea occur throughout *The Tempest*, a play that contains an unusual amount of compound nouns and adjectives invented by Shakespeare. This sequence of compound words is a selection of this distinctive language. (An ocean drum is a large tambour containing small metal balls. When the drum is moved, it makes a sound like the waves breaking on the shore.)

[Sound of an ocean drum]
Sea-sorrow
Wave-worn
Sea-change
Cloud-capp'd
Sea-storm
Thunder-stroke
Sea-swallow'd
Spell-stopp'd
[The gong is sounded, fading to silence]

Activity
This recital starts quietly, gradually gets louder, and then on the final line everyone 'freezes' at the sound of the gong. The silence is held as long as possible. The activity is started by the sound of an ocean drum recorded on a switch.

◆ EPISODE 5: PROSPERO

The Tempest ends in peace for everyone. These are some of Prospero's famous concluding lines describing the play, the theatre, and human life itself, as a dream:

> *Sssshhhh*
> Our revels now are ended
> We are such stuff
> As dreams are made on
> And our little life
> Is rounded with a sleep
> *Sssshhhh*

Activity
A quiet activity, beginning and ending with a 'Sssshhh', ends the workshop. A parachute is raised and lowered as the lines are spoken, and released on the final 'Sssshhhh', to cover everyone.

Twelfth Night

These two series of poetry workshops on Shakespeare's *Twelfth Night* were first performed with teenagers with severe and profound learning disabilities from Charlton School in Greenwich and Greenvale School in Lewisham (London), between October 2002 and April 2003. Each school had three series of workshops. The first series took place on stage at Shakespeare's Globe Theatre in October and November 2002, and consisted of the sub-plot of Malvolio's story. The second series of workshops also took place at the Globe, in January and February 2003, and consisted of the main plot of *Twelfth Night*. The third and final series of workshops was held in the Great Hall at Hall Place, a Tudor manor house in Bexley, in March and April 2003, when the two workshops were put together as one large workshop that could accommodate the double storyline of Shakespeare's play. The Charlton School group performed the third workshop at Hall Place, together with a group of children from a local mainstream school, so the workshops also served as an inclusion project.

◆ EPISODE 1: MAIN PLOT

The duke Orsino is in love with Olivia:

> If music be the food of love,
> Play on; give me excess of it
> That, surfeiting
> The appetite
> May sicken
> And so die
> [Music plays]
> Get off!

Activity
The opening lines of the play are followed by someone playing a small extract from a well-known piece of music (for example, from The Sound of Music*) on a kazoo. This is followed swiftly by everyone shouting out 'Get off!', or 'Enough!', or 'Put a sock in it!' Switch-users can have recorded bits of music on the kazoo to play.*

Episode 1: Sub-plot

Malvolio is a steward at the house of the Lady Olivia. Down in the kitchen, her maid Maria describes him to the others:

> Oh Malvolio
> He is a kind of puritan
> It is his grounds of faith
> That all that look on him
> Love him
> Oh yeah, right!

Activity

Malvolio (one or many) can move around inside the circle of participants – maybe wearing a black hat – admiring himself. The lines are spoken with everyone pointing at Malvolio, and then everyone joins with the final contemptuous 'Oh yeah, right!' Switch-users can play a Homer Simpson style 'Doh!'

◆ EPISODE 2: MAIN PLOT

Orsino sends his messenger Cesario (who is really Viola disguised as a man) to woo Olivia – she promptly falls in love with the messenger. Viola (ie, Cesario) leaves Olivia saying, in a deep voice, 'I am a gentleman'...

> 'I am a gentleman'
> I'll be sworn thou art
> Not so fast
> Soft, soft!
> How now!
> Even so quickly
> May one catch the plague?
> *Ooh young man!*

Activity

Olivia's lines, addressed to Cesario the messenger, are done with one or more people in the middle of the circle, surrounded by the other participants. The words can be spoken in the style of Harry Enfield and Kathy Burke playing two predatory old ladies trapping the milkman in the kitchen, using their catchphrase as a final line. As the lines are recited, everyone moves towards the people at the centre of the circle, stretching out their hands towards the 'young man' in the middle. (Harry Enfield and Kathy Burke were in a popular BBC comedy programme. In one sketch they played two elderly ladies who try to seduce the young and innocent milkman who delivers each morning.)

Episode 2: Sub-plot

Malvolio walks in the garden, admiring himself, followed by the others who call him names:

Here's an overweening rogue!
Fie on him, Jezebel!
Fire and brimstone!
Bolts and shackles!
Out, scab!
Sheep-biter!
Baaaa!

Activity

One or more participants are in the middle of the circle. As the lines are spoken in call and response, everyone moves slowly inwards towards the person or persons in the middle. The insults get louder and louder until the 'Out, scab!' line is shouted, which is followed by the quieter 'sheep biter', and then a really loud 'Baaaa!' Switch-users can have a quieter 'Baaaa' sound, or a giggle.

◆ EPISODE 3: MAIN PLOT

Viola is in love with Orsino, but cannot say anything because she is disguised as a man (ie, a 'poor monster'). Unknown to everyone, Viola's twin brother, Sebastian, is about to appear and confuse matters even more:

My master loves her dearly
I, poor monster
Fond as much on him
She, mistaken
Seems to dote on me.
What will become of this?
Aarrgghh!

Activity

This exchange starts slowly, and gradually gets faster and faster, until the pent-up frustration of the final line is shouted out by everyone. Lots of gestures, especially pointing, are used. For 'my master' (line 1), ie Orsino, we point at one chosen person, and then the other hand points at the 'her', ie Olivia, of line 1; for the 'I' of line 2, participants point to themselves with one hand, and then with the other to the 'him' of line 3, Orsino again. Then participants point to 'she' in line 4 (Olivia) and then themselves – the 'me' of line 5 – before screaming with confusion. It is easier than it sounds.

Episode 3: Sub-plot

Malvolio reads a fake letter and thinks that the lady Olivia is in love with him:

My lady loves me
My yellow stockings
Cross-gartered
I thank my stars
I am happy
I will smile
What dish o'poison
Ha ha ha!

Activity

Here is a chance for some melodramatic acting, with much wringing of hands and heavy sighing. The last two lines are called out by everyone, with the final laugh being either sarcastic or an over-the-top manic laugh in the style of the Wicked Witch from the film The Wizard Of Oz. *Switch-users can have sounds of smothered laughter, or any other suitable effect.*

◆ EPISODE 4: MAIN PLOT

Sebastian tells Olivia that she almost married a woman, but she is now going to be married to a maid (Viola, as a sister-in-law) and man (Sebastian, as husband):

You have been mistook
You would have been contracted
To a maid
Nor are you deceived
You are betroth'd
Both to a maid and man
Doh!

Activity

One or more Olivias can be in the centre of the circle, and as the lines are recited, everyone slowly moves towards the participants in the middle, as in Activity 2. The final line – Homer Simpson style – is done to express an idea something like, 'Stupid or what!'

Episode 4: Sub-plot
Malvolio goes to Olivia, repeats the contents of the letter, and shows his yellow legs.
Olivia screams:

Be not afraid of greatness
Some are born great
Some achieve greatness
Some have greatness
Thrust upon them
Yellow stockings!
Cross-gartered!
Aarrgghh!

Activity
The words of the letter can be called out in an eager and excited voice, while the final three lines are done in full shock-horror style, because, of course, Viola thinks he has gone completely mad and screams loudly. Switch-users can play a pantomime-style 'Oooohhhh!'

A song from Feste, the clown, to end the workshop:

What is love? 'Tis not hereafter
Present mirth hath present laughter
What's to come is still unsure
In delay there lies no plenty
Then come and kiss me, sweet and twenty
Youth's a stuff will not endure
Hooray!

Activity
This song can be done with or without musical instruments. We usually do it in a bright and breezy style with clapping and foot-stamping, etc. One morning on stage at the Globe in January, it was so cold that the Greenvale teenagers started to jump up and down on the spot as they began calling out the words. This turned into what may be a new art form of 'Shakespeare-pogo', a dance-poem recited while jumping energetically towards the centre in time for the final 'Hooray!'

Chapter 4

Charles Dickens

Charles Dickens

The following two stories by Charles Dickens have been used with a number of storytelling groups.

It is interesting to note that Charles Dickens became a hugely successful public performer of his own stories. His readings of extracts from his novels attracted enormous public interest, and these readings, especially of the murder of Nancy by Bill Sikes from *Oliver Twist*, were sensationally popular. As an oral storyteller, Dickens was apparently spellbinding:

'Dickens walked onto the platform with his book in hand. The audience then rose to its feet, cheering and applauding, and he could not proceed for several minutes. After he had finished the second of his readings, once more the audience burst into applause and cheering which lasted for several minutes. He had left the platform but had been recalled by the enthusiasm – almost the hysteria – of the audience several times.' And when Dickens was eventually forced to retire from public readings of his works, for reasons of health, at the close of his final reading, a witness described Dickens receiving 'a storm of cheering as I have never seen equalled in my life'. (Ackroyd, 1990, p1127)

It has been calculated that Dickens may have invented as many as two thousand characters in his stories. These vivid and grotesque characters – such as Fagin the thief, Mr Bumble the beadle, the menacing Bill Sikes, and Ebenezer Scrooge the moneylender – provide excellent material for storytelling activities.

Oliver Twist

This version of *Oliver Twist* contains 10 episodes, nine of which are named after characters in the book; the last activity is a summary of what happens to all the characters after the story, as is the final chapter in the novel. Each section contains a brief description of the character, using the original language of the book. Most of the activities also use some of the original language. All activities are done as call and response, and with the use of communication aids such as Big Macks and step-by-step communicators as required. The words are chanted rather than spoken, to accentuate the rhythm of the language. The final line of each of the activities is called out by everyone and is in italic type. Unless indicated otherwise, each response line is the same as the call line.

London is the location for most of the story of *Oliver Twist*, and the language of the novel may or may not reflect some of the London dialect of the day. Peter Ackroyd (1990) suggests that the slang in *Oliver Twist* and Dickens' other novels may be a comic invention by Dickens rather than the genuine slang of London. Some of the language used in the sequence of last lines comes from present day London and thereabouts: snippets from the British television soap *Eastenders*, and phrases that are often heard in the London area (eg, 'sorted!', 'that is well out of order!'). This provides a light-hearted connection between the language of today and the language of Dickens' London, real or imaginary, of the early nineteenth century. The novel has been printed and published in a huge variety of editions, and so to make it easier to find the extracts of quoted text, the chapter number is cited rather than a page number. The entire text of *Oliver Twist* is also available on the internet (http://www.bibliomania.com/Fiction/dickens/Oliver/index.html).

◆ EPISODE 1: OLIVER

'Oliver Twist's ninth birthday found him a pale thin child, somewhat diminutive in stature, and decidedly small in circumference' (Ch.2). He lives in a workhouse with several other children; they work hard and are always very hungry. Someone has to ask for more food. At supper time, Oliver gets up:

I take my spoon
I take my spoon
And my basin
And my basin
Rise from the table
Rise from the table
Go to the master
Go to the master

And I say
And I say
Please sir, I want some more
What?
Please sir, I want some more
What!
Please sir, I want some more
Throw him in the slammer!

Props

A wooden spoon and a wooden bowl. Choose ones that are quite different from mealtime utensils, to avoid confusion.

◆ EPISODE 2: MR BUMBLE

'Mr Bumble was a fat man, and a choleric' (Ch.2). He is one of the people in charge of the workhouse; he decides that Oliver is too much trouble and should be sold:

Oliver Twist for sale!
Oliver Twist for sale!
Not thirty pound
Not thirty pound
Not twenty pound
Not twenty pound
Not even ten
Not even ten
Not even five
Not even five
To you three quid
Done!
Sold!
Cor! wot a bargain!

Props

A wooden hammer as a gavel.

◆ EPISODE 3: THE ARTFUL DODGER

Oliver runs away to London and meets the Artful Dodger, whom Dickens describes (Ch.8) as follows (except for the last line!):

snub-nosed
snub-nosed

flat-browed
flat-browed
common-faced
common-faced
bow-legs
bow-legs
sharp eyes
sharp eyes
man's coat
man's coat
cuffs back
cuffs back
Artful Dodger?
Artful Dodger?
E's a geezer!

Props
A hat and scarf.

◆ EPISODE 4: FAGIN

The Artful Dodger takes Oliver to the gang's hide-out in Saffron Hill to meet Fagin, who has a 'villainous looking and repulsive face' (Ch.8). Fagin teaches Oliver how to be a pickpocket by stealing handkerchiefs or, as Fagin calls them, 'wipes' (Ch.9).

This activity mixes the language used by Fagin (words such as 'wipes', and phrases such as 'shan't us Oliver') with contemporary London slang ('schmatte' is material or cloth; 'tea leaf' is rhyming slang for 'thief', used because Oliver is unknowingly being taught to be a thief). On the second line, when saying the word 'Oliver', Fagin selects and points to someone in the group – as do the rest of the group in the response line – who then tries to pick Fagin's pocket, which has a large, glittery cloth hanging out of it. Winners can be Fagin the next time.

We'll have such fun
We'll have such fun
Shan't us Oliver
Shan't us Oliver
See this wipe
See this wipe
Nice bit of schmatte
Nice bit of schmatte
Can you take it?
Can you take it?

So I don't feel it
So I don't feel it
Is it gone?
Is it gone?
Didn't feel a thing!
Didn't feel a thing!
E's a proper tea leaf!

Props
A shiny piece of material to be the handkerchief.

◆ EPISODE 5: MR FANG

They go out to pick pockets, and Oliver gets caught. He is taken to Mr Fang, the police magistrate, 'a lean, long-backed, stiff-necked, middle-sized man' (Ch.11), who is in a very bad temper. He shouts at everyone. Mr Fang's words are taken directly from the book:

Who are you!
Oliver Twist
Swear this person!
He is sick
Hold your tongue sir!
Very sick
What's your name!
Really sick
Stuff and nonsense!
Now he's fainted
Clear the office!
Oi You! That's well out of order!

Props
Pen and paper (or, for those with an enthusiasm for authenticity, a goose quill and parchment!).

◆ EPISODE 6: MR GRIMWIG

Mr Grimwig was:

a stout old gentleman, rather lame in one leg, who was dressed in a blue coat, striped waistcoat, nankeen breeches and gaiters, and a broad-brimmed white hat, with the sides turned up with green... The ends of his white neckerchief were twisted into a ball about the size of an orange; the variety of shapes into which his countenance was twisted, defy description. He had the manner of screwing his head on one side when he spoke;

and of looking out of the corner of his eyes at the same time, which irresistibly reminded the beholder of a parrot (Ch.14).

Mr Grimwig only appears to be a grumpy old man, but really he is kind and considerate. Dickens, with a touch of genius, calls him Grimwig because his grimness, like a wig, is removable and reveals the kindly character underneath. Mr Grimwig makes out that Oliver is a bad boy, and says that if Oliver comes back from his errand he will eat his own head (Ch.14):

My name is Mr Grimwig
Hello Mr Him Big
No – my name is Mr Grimwig
Hello Mr Dim Fig
No – my name is Mr Grimwig
Hello Mr Limb Big
No – my name is Mr Grimwig
Hello Mr Gin Big
No – my name is Mr Grimwig and if Oliver Twist comes back I'll eat my head!
Oooh Tasty!!

Props
A hat, and a scarf or cravat.

◆ EPISODE 7: NANCY

Nancy, 'gorgeously attired, in a red gown, green boots, and yellow curl papers' (Ch.13) is one of the gang. She sees Oliver in the street, grabs him and takes him back to Fagin and his gang.

This call and response activity is a three-way exchange between Nancy, Oliver and the crowd:

Oh there you are – where have you been?
Who me? (Yes, you!)
Oh there you are – what are you like!
Who me? (Yes, you!)
Oh there you are – come home with me!
Who me? – (Yes, you!)
Oliver Twist?
Sorted!

Props
A shawl (or equivalent), and a handbag.

◆ EPISODE 8: BARNEY

Barney is also one of the gang: 'whose words, whether they came from the heart or not, made their way through the nose' (Ch.15). He meets the rest of the gang, and they plan a burglary. In the story, Dickens writes Barney's voice as if he has a cold (ie, Mister Sikes comes out as Bister Sikes), and so here the response part is the 'translation' of Barney's bunged up speech. The listeners get more and more irritated until they tell Barney to blow his nose, at which point the cold in his head mysteriously transfers itself to them!

> Bister Sikes
> *Mister Sikes*
> Dice to beet you
> *Nice to meet you*
> Bister Sikes
> *Mister Sikes*
> Do cub id
> *Do come in*
> Bister Sikes
> *Mister Sikes*
> Where we goid?
> *Where are we going?*
> Bister Sikes
> *Blow your nose!!*
> [Everyone loudly blows raspberries]
> Mmmuch better, thank you
> *Dat's OK Bardey!*

Props
Lots of handkerchiefs (one for everyone if possible).

◆ EPISODE 9: BILL SIKES

Bill Sikes is bad news:

> He had a brown hat on his head, and a dirty belcher handkerchief round his neck;
> with the long frayed ends of which he smeared the beer from his face as he spoke.
> He disclosed, when he had done so, a broad heavy countenance with a beard of three
> days' growth, and two scowling eyes; one of which displayed various parti-coloured
> symptoms of having been recently damaged by a blow (Ch.13).

Bill Sikes forces Oliver to take part in a burglary (Ch.12) and says the words below. In the attempted burglary, Oliver gets shot. (*Note:* A belcher handkerchief was the term used in the early nineteenth century to describe a coloured handkerchief that was worn around the neck.)

Now listen you
Now listen you
Take this light
Take this light
Up the stairs
Up the stairs
Along the hall
Along the hall
To the door
To the door
Now
Now
(A loud bang on a drum)
E's copped it!

Props
A torch, and a scarf or mask.

◆ EPISODE 10: THE END

After lots of adventures, everything ends happily for Oliver. The last chapter describes what happens to some of the people in the story:

Nancy
Bought it
Bill Sikes
Swung
Barney
Doesn't say
Fagin
Hung
Mr Grimwig
Bright and cheerful
Mr Fang
Who knows
Artful Dodger
In the nick
Mr Bumble
Workhouse
And Oliver Twist
Lived happily ever after
Ah bless!

A Christmas Carol

This adaptation was written to include Joshua (eight years old), who is blind and has complex needs, into peer-group activities. The call and response, with the rhythmic language, enabled Joshua to participate as an equal. The single prop used in the story is a large, white, glittery blanket, available from many fabric shops.

◆ EPISODE 1: SCROOGE

It is Christmas Eve, and everyone is having fun except Scrooge, a miser. When anyone mentions Christmas, he says 'Bah, humbug!' While everyone is going out with friends and family to celebrate Christmas Eve, and to prepare for Christmas Day, he goes home alone to his cold and dreary house:

> Scrooge is my name
> *Scrooge is your name*
> Loads of money!
> *Loads of money!*
> You want presents?
> *We want presents!*
> Very funny!
> *Very funny*
> Christmas?
> *Humbug!*

Activity
After the line 'Christmas', everyone yells 'Humbug'. As an additional activity, Scrooge can then fall asleep over his plate of treasure, and people can take it in turns to creep up and take something. If Scrooge wakes up, he can shout 'go away' again. Winners can become Scrooge. Near Christmas time, the phrase 'You want presents?' can be 'Christmas presents?'

◆ EPISODE 2: MARLEY'S GHOST

Scrooge, alone in the darkness of his home, sees the ghost of Jacob Marley, his former business partner, who appears in chains: 'I wear the chain I forged in life', in other words, out of greed. He tells Scrooge, 'You will be haunted by Three Spirits.' These are the spirits of Christmas Past, Christmas Present and Christmas Yet To Come:

I'm a ghost and I can see you
[everyone in ghostly chant] *eeee – oooo*
I'm a ghost and I might get you
[everyone in ghostly chant] *eeee – oooo*
BOO!

Activity

On the 'BOO!', the ghost grabs somebody, or throws a blanket over them. Someone else can then be the ghost. (We have had great fun with an alternative version: 'I'm the ghost of Jacob Marley', 'eeee – oooo', ' On my seven fifty Harley, VVROOOMM!' Marley's ghost then noisily departs on his authentic early Victorian motorbike.)

◆ EPISODE 3: THE FIRST OF THE THREE SPIRITS – MR FEZZIWIG'S BALL

The first spirit takes Scrooge back into his past, where they see his fomer boss, Mr Fezziwig, a jolly and generous man. They see lots of seasonal merrymaking, including Mr Fezziwig's Ball, where he leads everyone in a dance to a fiddler that Dickens describes as being 'tuned like fifty stomach-aches.'

Mister Fezziwig
Likes to party
Mister Fezziwig
Starts to dance:
Claps his hands
[clap three times]
Stamps his feet
[stamp three times]
Knocks on wood
[knock three times]
And one more time
Claps his hands
[clap three times]
Stamps his feet
[stamp three times]
Knocks on wood
[knock three times]
And shouts Hooray
Hooray!

◆ EPISODE 4: THE SECOND OF THE THREE SPIRITS – BOB CRATCHIT'S CHRISTMAS DINNER

The second spirit shows Scrooge how people are celebrating Christmas Eve. Bob Cratchit – one of Scrooge's employees – and his family, despite their poverty, are enjoying their Christmas dinner of roasted goose, mashed potatoes, apple sauce, and a Christmas pudding 'like a speckled cannon ball', followed by apples and oranges, roasted chestnuts, and a drink of 'hot stuff from the jug' that was probably mulled wine. They toast Scrooge, despite the fact that he is mean and horrible:

Roasted goose
Roasted goose
Sage and onion
Sage and onion
Mashed potato
Mashed potato
Christmas pudding
Christmas pudding
Apples and oranges
Apples and oranges
Roasted
Roasted
Chest
Chest
Nuts!

Activity

This is a call and response routine that uses the food items described by Dickens in the story. It starts slowly, gets faster, and then slows down until everyone shouts out the last part of the last line together (Nuts!) We did calls and responses twice each for each line (eg, Roasted goose, Roasted goose, Roasted goose, Roasted goose).

◆ **EPISODE 5: THE LAST OF THE SPIRITS – SAVING TINY TIM**

The third spirit is of Christmas Yet To Come; he shows Scrooge the future. In the Cratchit household, Tiny Tim's place by the fire is empty. No one remembers Scrooge. It is time for Scrooge to make his moral choice:

If Tiny Tim
If Tiny Tim
Does not get well
Does not get well
Then Mister Scrooge
Then Mister Scrooge
Will disappear
Will disappear
Just
Just
Like
Like
This
Ahhh

Activity
The stress in the rhythm of this game's call and response – on the second and fourth beat of each line – is the reverse of that in Episode 1. Try it with the lights out, and with the words spoken quietly, as a contrast to the preceding game. When saying the final line, a blanket is thrown over a chosen victim. Try sweeping the blanket over the group as the words are chanted – who will be the next victim?

◆ **EPISODE 6: THE END OF IT**

Dickens uses the words 'The End Of It' as the title of the final chapter in the story. This activity is not really a game but a way of finishing the session. Scrooge wakes up and is changed by his dreams: he decides to become kind and generous, so he shares out his tray of treasures (now magically containing sweets) with everyone, saying 'please take one of these!' Alternatively, the group leader can shake hands with everyone, and say 'happy Christmas' or some other appropriate greeting.

Chapter 5

Poetry and Song

One thousand years of poetry

This poetry project started with a group of students with severe and profound learning disabilities. It contains six pieces of English poetry from the tenth to the twentieth century, at approximately 200-year intervals, and represents a millennium of poetry and an illustration of a thousand-year development of the English language. This chapter describes how these poems are being used, in a multisensory and interactive style, with children and teenagers with severe and profound learning disabilities.

The earliest written evidence for the existence of the *Beowulf* poem is from a British Museum manuscript that dates from about AD 1000 (Porter, 1995), although it may have existed in oral versions for many years before that date. It can be regarded as one of the first pieces of English literature, even though it has no resemblance to modern English. The second and third poems, both of which are anonymous, show the emergence of recognisable modern English. The fourth poem is a re-setting of the story of Joseph, using the language of the King James Bible of 1611. The fifth, by Coleridge, is an extract of a famous, and famously enigmatic, poem.

Poem 1: Tenth Century – Beowulf

This extract from *Beowulf* is an adaptation of a literal translation (Porter, 1995) that uses individual lines of text (from lines 100 to 850) which give an abbreviated account of the fight between Beowulf and Grendel. This is in an attempt to preserve something of the Old English rhythm and metre, as well as the intensity and richness of the original language, and at the same time, to maintain a strong narrative. The language in *Beowulf* has been celebrated for its 'kennings', the poetical compound nouns that occur frequently thoroughout the narrative. For example, the sea is referred to as a 'whale-road', 'sea-street' and 'brine-path'; the monster Grendel is the 'march-stepper' (literally the walker through marshes), 'sin-scourer' and 'shadow-walker' (he comes in the night for his victims); human blood is 'sword-juice'. In the battle between Grendel and Beowulf, Grendel's joint of arm and shoulder is a 'bone-lock'; elsewhere the human body is described as a 'flesh-cloak' and, in particular, as a 'bone-house'. This vivid phrase from the tenth century by the *Beowulf* poet resurfaces, 1,000 years later, in the poetry of Seamus Heaney (1996).

Sometimes, to heighten the atmosphere of menace, we project a colour slide of Goya's *Saturno* on to the wall. This is a very powerful and disturbing picture that graphically illustrates Grendel's predatory activities. Another simple way of adding to the atmosphere is to use the chorus line of 'Grendel shadow walker' in its Old English version of 'Grendel sceadugenga'.

> Grendel was the fiend in hell
> Ghastly spirit, wretched creature
> Thing of malice grim and greedy
> Grim lone-walker, shadow-walker.
> > *Grendel shadow-walker*

> And the monster mauling was
> In dark-death shadow, old and young
> Thence back went in plunder proud
> Homeward faring with the death-feast.
> > *Grendel shadow-walker*

> Beowulf spoke, I shall achieve
> A daring deed or else death-day
> Then came from moor, under mist-hills
> Monster Grendel, cursed spirit.
> > *Grendel shadow-walker*

Then his heart laughed, dreadful monster,
He snatched a sleeping warrior
Bit bone-locks, drank blood from veins
Unliving man entire devoured.
Grendel shadow-walker

Took then with hand – he reached for him
The hand of Beowulf
He had not met on middle-earth
In other man a hand-grip harder.
Grendel shadow-walker

Huge wound seen on dreadful monster
Sinews broke; burst bone-locks
To Beowulf was glory given
Grendel thence must life-sick flee.
Grendel shadow-walker

Grendel's severed arm and shoulder
Grendel's grip hung on the wall
There was blood in water welling
Grendel, death-doomed, life laid down.
Grendel shadow-walker

Poem 2: Thirteenth Century – a Lyke-wake Dirge

It has been suggested that, in its oral version, this poem dates from the twelfth or thirteenth century. 'Lyke' is an Old English word meaning 'corpse', and so a lyke-wake dirge was a song of lament. The use of the word 'lyke' may make the poem older in origin than has been estimated. The poem has been set to music, and sung by a number of singers and musicians. The second and fourth lines of each verse are the same; and the poem lends itself very well to call and response, where an individual speaks lines one and three, and the chorus takes lines two and four.

This ae night, this ae night
Every night and all
Fire and flood and candle light
And Christ receive thy soul.

When thou from hence away art passed
Every night and all
To Whinny-Muir thou com'st at last
And Christ receive thy soul.

If ever thou gavest hosen and shoon
Every night and all
Sit thee down and put them on
And Christ receive thy soul.

If hosen and shoon thou ne'er gavest none
Every night and all
The whins shall prick thee to the bare bones
And Christ receive thy soul.

From Whinny-Muir when thou mayest pass
Every night and all
To Brig o' Dread thou com'st at last
And Christ receive thy soul.

From Brig o' Dread when thou mayest pass
Every night and all
To Purgatory fire thou com'st at last
And Christ receive thy soul.

If ever thou gavest meat or drink
Every night and all
The fire shall never make thee shrink
And Christ receive thy soul.

If meat or drink thou gavest none
Every night and all
The fire will burn thee to the bare bone
And Christ receive thy soul.

This ae night, this ae night
Every night and all
Fire and flood and candle light
And Christ receive thy soul.

(from Herbert, 1997, pp3–4)

Poem 3: Fifteenth Century – Swarte-smeked Smethes (Smoke-blackened Smiths)

This anonymous poem, from about 1440, is a complaint about noisy neighbours. The writer complains about the smoke-blackened smiths (the 'swarte-smeked smethes'), the neighbours, who work non-stop through the night and make it impossible to sleep. It is described as being remarkable because of 'its conspicuous verbs and its stress and clash of consonants' (Davies, 1978, p350), and it is clearly a poem for a hearing audience rather than a reading one. In our classroom performances we begin with everyone knocking or stamping four beats, with the fourth beat stronger than the preceding three. This is repeated, and then followed by the chanting of the first half of the first line of the poem: swarte-smeked smethes *knock* – to which the response is the second half of the first line: smatered with smoke, *knock*. This rhythm establishes a powerful momentum, and helps people to pronounce the unfamiliar-sounding words. The storyteller then says each three-line section, via a communication aid when necessary, after which everyone repeats the chorus. We began by practising the first few lines, and gradually added more until we were using the entire poem. With the addition of a few tambours and beaters, and a few minutes practice of the pronunciation of the words (all initial consonants are pronounced, and so *gnawen* and *gnacchen* really do begin with a 'g'; real purists can even pronounce the 'k' in *knock*), the result can be very effective.

> Knock knock, knock, knock;
> *knock, knock, knock, knock*
> Swarte-smeked smethes, (knock)
> *smatered with smoke (knock)*
>
> Drive me to deth with den of here dintes
> Swich nois on nightes ne herd men never,
> What knavene cry and clatering of knockes
>
> The cammede kongons cryen after 'Col! col!'
> And blowen here bellowes that all here brain brestes
> 'Huf, puf', seith that on, 'Haf, paf' that other
>
> They spitten and sprawlen and spellen many spelles
> They gnawen and gnacchen, they grones togidere
> And holden hem hote with here hard hamers

Of a bole hide ben here barm-felles
Here shankes ben shakeled for the fere-flunderes
Heavy hameres they han that hard ben handled

Stark strokes they striken on a steled stocke
'Lus, bus, las, bas,' rowten by rowe
Swiche dolful a dreme the Devil it todrive!

The maister longeth a litil and lasheth a lesse
Twineth hem twain and toucheth a treble
'Tik, tak, hic, hac, tiket, taket, tik, tak

Lus, bus, lus, das.' Swich lif they leden,
Alle clothermeres, Christ hem give sorwe!
May no man for brenwateres on night han his rest.

Translation

Smoke-blackened smiths, begrimed with smoke, drive me to death with din of their blows: such noise by nights no man ever heard, what crying of workmen and clattering of blows!

The crooked (snub-nosed?) changelings cry out for 'Coal! Coal!', and blow their bellows fit to burst their brains. 'Huf puf,' says that one, 'Haf paf,' the other.

They spit and sprawl and tell many tales, they gnaw and gnash, they groan together, and keep themselves hot with their hot hammers.

Of bull hide are their leather aprons, their legs are protected against the fiery sparks. Heavy hammers they have that are handled hard.

Strong blows they strike on an anvil of steel, 'Lus, bus, las, bas,' they crash in turn. May the devil put an end to so miserable a racket!

The master smith lengthens a little piece of iron, hammers a smaller piece, twists the two together, and strikes a treble note, 'tik, tak, hic, hac, tiket, taket, tik, tak'.

'Lus, bus, las, bas.' Such a life they lead, all smiths who clothe horses in iron armour, may heaven punish them! For smiths who burn water no man can sleep at night.

(*Note:* Blacksmiths are described in the poem as *clothmeres* and *brenwateres*: clothmeres are those who clothe horses in iron armour, and brenwateres are those who burn water – ie, they cool hot iron in water. The description of some of the workers as crooked, or maybe snub-nosed changelings – it is difficult to be sure of the original meanings of the words – may have been insulting.

Poem 4: Seventeenth century – the Story of Joseph (Genesis, Ch.37–45), from the King James Bible of 1611

The anonymous writer of the opening note to a recent edition of the book of Genesis suggests that:

> The authorised King James Version of the Bible, translated between 1603–11, co-incided with an extraordinary flowering of English literature. This version, more than any other, and possibly more than any other work in history, has had an influence in shaping the language we speak and write today. (Rose, 1998)

The introduction to the same edition of Genesis, by Steven Rose, suggests that, for storytelling, Genesis is where it all starts:

> The Creation, Eden, Adam and Eve, the Fall, Cain and Abel, the Flood and Noah's Ark, Babel's Tower, Abraham and the Sacrifice of Isaac, Jacob and his ladder, Sodom and Gomorrah, Joseph with his Coat of Many Colours – and with Potiphars Wife – Pharoah's dream of the seven fat and seven lean cattle. The images speak to us through centuries of painting, sculpture, novels and poems... And all within 65 pages... A miracle of terse story telling.... (Rose, 1998, pviii)

Terse is indeed the word: many people might argue that a retelling of the story of Joseph becomes a matter of not what to rephrase but what to omit. This retelling uses the language of the King James Bible with very little alteration, but omits the verses about the interpretation of Pharoah's dream (Genesis, Ch.39) and instead concentrates on the story of Joseph and his family.

In order to make the performance of this story as clear as possible, the syllables that are stressed are in bold type. We worked on the Genesis material for several weeks. In week one we did Section 1 four times; in week two we did Section 1 once, and then Section 2 twice; in week three we did Sections 1, 2 and then 3, and so on, until we went through the entire piece. This took place in the school hall, with all the participants in a circle and with the lights out; in the middle of the circle was a four-metre square piece of bright yellow fake fur (the desert) on which was placed a fibre-optic spray (the camp fire). Switch-users can play desert sound effects, such as whistling wind, goat bells, etc, to add to the atmosphere and to increase opportunities for participation. The text may not at first sight appear to be accessible, but it is easier than it might look!

1: Genesis, Chapter 37

Joseph **was** the **son** of **Ja**cob
Jacob **dwelt** with**in** the **coun**try
Where his **fa**ther **was** a **stra**nger
In the Land of Canaan

Born to **Ja**cob **in** his **old** age
Jacob **loved** his **son** called **Jo**seph
More than **all** his **oth**er **chil**dren
In the Land of Canaan

All the **broth**ers **hate**d **Jo**seph
With his **coat** of **man**y **col**ours
For his **dreams** and **for** his **stor**ies
In the Land of Canaan

'What **is** this **dream** that **thou** hast **dreamed**?
Shall **we** bow **down** our**selves** to **thee**?'
And **so** his **broth**ers **en**vied **him**
In the Land of Canaan

Then they **said** to **one** an**oth**er:
'**Look** this **dream**er **com**eth **to** us
Shed no **blood** but **let** us **sell** him'
In the Land of Canaan

Took the **coat** of **man**y **col**ours
Dipped the **coat** in **blood** of **goat** and
Brought it **to** their **fath**er **Ja**cob
In the Land of Canaan

'This **have** we **found**' and **Ja**cob **saw**
'**Jo**seph **has** been **rent** in **piec**es'
Thus his **fa**ther **wept** for **him**
In the Land of Canaan

2: Genesis, Chapters 39–41

Joseph **was** brought **down** to **E**gypt
Potiphar be**came** his **mas**ter
And he **made** him over**seer**

In the Land of Egypt

Pharoah **sent** and **called** to **Jo**seph
Pharoah **then** said **un**to **Jo**seph:
'**Thou** canst **und**er**stand** a **dream**

In the Land of Egypt

In my **dream** the **sev**en **fat** kine
Were de**voured** by **sev**en **lean** kine
No mag**i**cian **can** de**clare** it

In the Land of Egypt

Joseph **said**, 'The **dream** of **Phar**oah
Tells of **sev**en **years** of **plen**ty
Next come **sev**en **years** of **fam**ine'

In the Land of Egypt

Set a **wise** man **o**ver **E**gypt
He will **gath**er **all** the **food** and
Store the **food** a**gainst** the **fam**ine'

In the Land of Egypt

Pharoah **then** said **un**to **Jo**seph:
'**There** is **none** so **wise** as **thou** art'
Pharoah **then** made **Jo**seph **ru**ler

In the Land of Egypt

Joseph **gath**ered **up** the **corn** to
Store the **food** a**gainst** the **fam**ine
Hunger **came** but **there** was **food**

In the Land of Egypt

3: Genesis, Chapter 42

Then said **Jacob to** his **chil**dren:
'**I** have **heard** of **corn** in **E**gypt
Buy for **us** that **we** may **live**'

                               And they did not know him

Joseph's **bro**ther **Ben**jamin
Jacob **sent** not **with** his **breth**ren
Lest some **mis**chief **should** be**fall** him

                               And they did not know him

So the **broth**ers **came** to **Jo**seph
They bowed **down** them**selves** be**fore** him
Joseph **saw** his **breth**ren, **knew** them

                               And they did not know him

Said he **to** them: '**Are** you **spies**?'
'**Nay**,' said **they**, 'we **are** twelve **breth**ren
With our **fa**ther **is** the **young**est'

                               And they did not know him

'**I** shall **know** if **ye** are **true** men
Bring your **young**est **broth**er **to** me
Then **I** shall **know** ye **are** no **spies**'

                               And they did not know him

Joseph **filled** their **sacks** with **corn** and
Put their **mon**ey **in** their **sacks** and
So they **came** a**gain** to **Ja**cob

                               And they did not know him

Told him **of** the **words** of **Jo**seph
Then said **Jacob to** his **chil**dren:
'**My son** shall **not** go **down** with **you**'

                               And they did not know him

4: Genesis, Chapter 43

Then did **Jacob speak** un**to** them
When **they** had **eat**en **all** the **corn:**
'**If** it **must** be **so** now, **do** this,

Go again to Egypt

Benja**m**in my **young**est **son.**
God Al**might**y **give** you **mer**cy
Go ag**ain** un**to** the **man**.'

Go again to Egypt

So they **took** the **dou**ble **mo**ney
Benja**m**in, the **young**est **broth**er
Came ag**ain** to **Jo**seph's **house**

Go again to Egypt

And **said:** '**O Sir** it **came** to **pass**
We **op**ened **up** our **sacks** of **food**
And **found** our **mon**ey **in** full **weight**'

Go again to Egypt

Joseph **said:** 'Peace **be** to **you**,
The **God** of your **father**
Hath **given** you **trea**sure **in** your **sacks**

Go again to Egypt

And **is** your **fa**ther **yet** a**live?**
And is **this** thy **young**er **broth**er?
Now **God** be **gra**cious **un**to **thee**'

Go again to Egypt

And the **breth**ren **sat** be**fore** him
Here the **first**born **here** the **young**est,
They **ate** and **drank** and **were** at **peace**.

Go again to Egypt

5: Genesis, Chapter 44

Joseph **said:** 'Fill **sacks** with **food**
Put my **cup**, the **sil**ver **cup**
In the **sack**'s mouth **of** the **young**est
Who is lord of Egypt

Up and **foll**ow after **them**
Say **un**to **them** "Is **it** not **this**
The **cup** in **which** my **lord** doth **drink?**"
Who is lord of Egypt

So **he** with **whom** the **cup** is **found**
Henceforth **shall** be **Jo**seph's **ser**vant
And ye **shall** be **blame**less.'
Who is lord of Egypt

They **took** down **ev**ery **man** his **sack**
They **op**ened **ev**ery **man** his **sack**
The **cup** was **found** with **Ben**jamin
Who is lord of Egypt

They **came** to **Jo**seph's **house;** he **said:**
'**He** shall **be** my **ser**vant – **you** –
Go **you** in **peace to** your **fa**ther
Who is lord of Egypt

'We **have** a **fa**ther **an** old **man**
We **may** not **see** the **old** man's **face**
Ex**cept** our **young**est **bro**ther **with** us
Who is lord of Egypt

Now I **pray** thee **let** him **go**
How **shall** I **go** up **to** my **fa**ther
If **Ben**jamin be **not** with **me?**'
Who is lord of Egypt

6: Genesis, Chapter 45

Joseph **could** not **keep** from **cry**ing
Wept al**oud**, said **to** his **breth**ren:
'**I am Joseph**
Joseph son of Jacob

I am **Jo**seph; **I am** your **bro**ther
Whom ye **did** sell **in**to **E**gypt
Be not **grie**ved, nor **be** not **an**gry
Joseph son of Jacob

It **was** not **you** that **sent** me **here**
But **God** who **made** me **govern**or
Throughout **all** the **land** of **E**gypt
Joseph son of Jacob

Haste **ye** and **go** up **to** my **fa**ther
God hath **made** me **lord** of **E**gypt
Come **down** to **me** and **tarry** **not**
Joseph son of Jacob

It **is** my **mouth** that **speak**eth **to** you
Tell my **fa**ther **of** my **glo**ry
Ye shall **haste** and **bring** him **hith**er'
Joseph son of Jacob

Pharaoh **said:** 'Come **un**to **me**
The **good** of **all** the **land** is **yours.**
Bring your **fa**ther, **bring** him **here.**'
Joseph son of Jacob

And **Ja**cob **said:** 'It **is** en**ough.**
Jos**eph** my **son** is **yet** al**ive**
I **will** see **him** be**fore** I **die.**'
Joseph son of Jacob

Poem 5: Eighteenth Century – Kubla Khan by Samuel Taylor Coleridge

Kubla Khan has been an object of reverence among writers and critics since it first appeared in the 1798 edition of *The Lyrical Ballads* co-written with William Wordsworth. John Livingstone Lowes, an eminent Coleridge critic, suggested in an essay written in 1927, concerning the concluding section of the poem, that 'Nobody in his waking senses could have fabricated those amazing eighteen lines' (Lowes, 1978, p331), and rather stoically concluded that 'Kubla Khan is as near enchantment, I suppose, as we are likely to come in this dull world' (Lowes, 1978, p374). Here are 'those amazing eighteen lines' that we have performed in a darkened room while moving slowly around in a circle, with the group leader in the middle holding a candle or torch. It is a simple method of making a powerful poem even more atmospheric.

> A damsel with a dulcimer
> In a vision once I saw
> It was an Abyssinian maid,
> And on her dulcimer she played
> Singing of Mount Abora.
> Could I revive within me
> Her symphony and song
> To such deep delight 'twould win me
> That with music loud and long
> I would build that dome in air,
> That sunny dome! Those caves of ice!
> And all who heard should see them there,
> And all should cry, beware! beware!
> His flashing eyes, his floating hair!
> Weave a circle round him thrice
> And close your eyes with holy dread
> For he on honeydew hath fed
> And drunk the milk of paradise.

Sea shanties

This collection of sea shanties is taken from Stuart Frank's *Sea Chanteys and Sailors' Songs* (Frank, 2001). Sea shanties allow for improvisation, and accordingly this collection has been personalised for the individuals in the group, each of whom has their 'own' shanty that has been adapted to include their own name (all names have been changed).

BONEY

Tony was a warrior
Away, ay, yah!
A harrier, a terrier
Jean Fran-swah!

Tony fought the Russians
Away, ay, yah!
Then he fought the Prussians
Jean Fran-swah!

Moscow was a-blazing
Away, ay, yah!
And Tony was a-raging
Jean Fran-swah!

Tony went to Waterloo
Away, ay, yah!
There he got his overthrow
Jean Fran-swah!

Tony!

SHALLOW BROWN

A Yankee ship came down the river
Sandy, Sandy
A Yankee ship with a Yankee skipper
Sandy, Sandy
And who do you think was master of her?
Sandy, Sandy
And what do you think they had for dinner
Sandy, Sandy
A parrot's tail and monkey liver

Sandy!

PAY ME MY MONEY DOWN

I thought I heard our captain say
Pay me Joshua, pay me
Tomorrow is our sailing day
Pay me Joshua, pay me
The very next day we crossed the bar
Pay me Joshua, pay me
He hit me on the head with an iron spar
Pay me Joshua, pay me
I wish I was Mr Jackson's son
Pay me Joshua, pay me
Sit on the fence and watch work done
Pay me Joshua, pay me

Joshua!

REUBEN RANZO

Oh poor old Reuben Ranzo
Memet, boys, Memet
Oh pity poor Reuben Ranzo
Memet, boys, Memet

Oh Ranzo was no sailor
Memet, boys, Memet
So he shipped on board a whaler
Memet, boys, Memet

He washed once in a fortnight
Memet, boys, Memet
He said it was his birthright
Memet, boys, Memet

The captain was a good man
Memet, boys, Memet
Took Ranzo to his cabin
Memet, boys, Memet

He gave him wine and water
Memet, boys, Memet
Introduced him to his daughter
Memet, boys, Memet

Now he sails upon the water
Memet, boys, Memet
Captain Ranzo gives the orders
Memet, boys, Memet

Memet!

HAUL AWAY, JOE

Oh once I was in Ireland
A-diggin' turf and taties
We'll haul away Michelle!
But now I'm in a limejuice ship
A-hauling on the braces
We'll haul away Michelle!

King Louis was the King of France
Before the Re-vo-lu-tion
We'll haul away Michelle!
But then he got his head cut off
Which spoiled his Con-sti-tu-tion
We'll haul away Michelle!

St Patrick was a gentleman
He came from decent people
We'll haul away Michelle!
He built a church in Dublin Town
And on it put a steeple
We'll haul away Michelle!

Michelle!

JOHNNY BOKER

Oh do my Johnny Boker
Mei Lee!
Come rock and roll me over
Mei Lee!

Do, my Johnny Boker
Mei Lee!
The skipper is a rover
Mei Lee!

Do, my Johnny Boker
Mei Lee!
The mate he's never sober
Mei Lee!

Do, my Johnny Boker
Mei Lee!
The bosun is a so'ger
Mei Lee!

Mei Lee!

Chapter 6

Grimm Versions: Stories by the Brothers Grimm

Red Riding Hood – the Wolf's story

This story came about by chance. We were talking in school one day about 'Little Red Riding Hood' and how the story can be presented in so many different ways. For example, there is the familiar and rather comfortable fairy tale that is used in so many homes and schools, as well as the darker, more adult version by the late Angela Carter, and the quite scary film by Neil Jordan. Someone jokingly remarked that the Wolf gets a bad press simply by being a wolf, and so this version came about.

I want to eat
Red Riding Hood
Her Granny too
They'll taste so good
Sweet and sour
What a treat
I'm no bad wolf
I just need meat

Jugged hare, giblets
And loin chop
Steak tartare
Oh stop, stop, stop!

My granddaughter
A pretty sight!
Do you have time
To stay for a bite?
Thank you Granny
I think I will
I've got a bit
Of time to kill

Salt beef, biltong
Spare rib roast
Tripe and heart
Brains on toast

I have to say
She wasn't bad
Not the toughest
Granny I've had
Swallowed whole
So there's no waste
She leaves a subtle
Aftertaste

Liver and kidney
Hand and belly
Then rump steak
And marrowbone jelly

Here comes pudding
What a treat
Come in my dear
You are the sweet
Oh yes, it's me
You're quite a catch
So bottoms up
And down the hatch

Trotters and hock
And then lamb stew
And a piece of tail
A dream come true

No, not very nice
So sickly sweet
I just don't like
That kind of meat
They're coming back
Oh no, too late
I'm going to
Regurgitate

Head and neck end
Leg, blade bone
Then one spare rib
All on its own

Now the hunter's
Chasing me
Maybe I should
Taste and see
If it's his meat
That I prefer
He'd make a lovely
Beef chasseur

A turkey mince
Veal escalope
Faggots with brawn
I live in hope.

Cinderella – an epilogue by the Ugly Sisters

I had taken a group of pupils to The Churchill Theatre in Bromley (south east London) for an interactive performance of the story of 'Cinderella', using the script in this book. After the workshop, one of the teenagers asked what had happened to the Ugly Sisters after Cinderella and the Prince got married. No-one seemed to know, so I thought we could make up a story and exploit the interest in films shown by both staff and pupils.

Cinderella
That little creep
Swept the prince
Right off his feet
They got married
It's just not right
We're left at home
Not a man in sight

So we'll indulge
Ourselves, you see,
In a panto
Fantasy
An exercise
To set things right
We'll make our prince
By composite

We'll do a tour
Of Hollywood
Drooling over
The great and good
Then cut and paste
A Man Divine
Just like Doctor
Frankenstein

Next we will make
Our decision
On whom to make
The first incision
From each one
We'll make a start
By cutting off
A leading part

So: first of all
A pair of feet
Orlando Bloom's
Look quite neat
And then the legs
Of Kevin Spacey
Cos we've heard that
He's quite racy

Then Daniel Craig
We'll take his trunk
Double O Seven
Oh what a hunk!
And in the arms
Of Colin Firth
We'd surely get
Our money's worth

Lovely hands
We can transplant
From the splendid
Hugh Grant
And if he needs
To scratch an itch
Fingers from
John Malkovich

On Daniel's trunk
I think we'll go
For the head
Of Russell Crowe
Placed upon
A nice slim neck
That we'll take from
Ben Affleck

But this is too
Complicated!
And we will be
Incriminated!
Our scheme is mad
Just plain loony
Why don't we just
Take George Clooney?

Rumpelstiltskin – a case study in anger management

One of the several endings to this story is that Rumpelstiltskin, furious that his name has been discovered, actually rips himself in half. I wanted to explore the darker side of folk tales and then try to discuss with pupils how they might cope with anger without resorting to such extremes as Rumpelstiltskin.

Psychiatry
That's what they said
I had a bad place
In my head
Anger management
My shrink told me
I need Behaviour
Therapy

Because Mum and Dad
To their shame
Gave me this
Revolting name
And I really
Got the hump
When we went out
Dad called me 'Rump'

Every time
I hear my name
I feel disgust
Anger and shame
To discuss
Repercussions
It's twice weekly
Group discussions

There was this girl
At our meeting
Had a problem
Needed treating
And when I knew
After I met her
That I could help her
I felt better

In just one night
She had been told
To spin all this
Straw to gold
For human beings
That's just not on
She's being used
And put upon

But this is
A dwarfish art
It calms my nerves
And warms my heart
A practical
Activity
Like Occupational
Therapy

Well, my dear
Like you, I am
On a behavioural
Programme
I'll make your gold
But there's a fee
It will cost you
Your baby

She got upset
But gave consent
Then I got over
Confident
Keep your baby
If you win this game
Three guesses for
My real name

Then I went home
In a dream
Contemplating
My clever scheme
I will be needed
Every day
My anger will
Just fade away

Deep breathing
Much enhanced
By this fantastic
Yogic trance
I have come through
Now I can say
Rumpelstiltskin
It's all OK

Some guttersnipe
Overheard my name
And told the girl
My secret shame
And so when we
Met next day
My tragedy
Was set to play

What makes us want
Things to get worse?
Maybe The Imp
Of The Perverse
Alright my dear
Decision time
Just three guesses
Then he is mine

Mister D'Arcy?
Sorry no
D'Artagnan?
Just one more go
My final guess:
I'm going to win!
How about
Rumpelstiltskin?

I smashed my foot
Right through the floor
Grabbed the other
Then what's more
I tore myself
Right in half
And gave the world
A right good laugh

So then my shrink
She wrote a book
From my case notes
Go have a look
The book is on
The library shelf
Entitled
The Divided Self.

Snow White – a story about apples

We had just finished a workshop on 'Snow White', using the script in this book, when one of the staff asked if the Wicked Queen had a name, to which someone quickly replied that, disguised as a Granny, she could have been Granny Smith. So this story came about: an alternative version of the story of Snow White, set in New York, and using many types of apples as a running joke.

◆ EPISODE 1: GRANNY SMITH, THE WICKED QUEEN

Yo mirror!
Tell me straight
Is there a girl
That I should hate
Who's number one?
Don't mess with me
Americans don't
Do irony

On reflection
I can tell
Your situation's
Far from well
The best apple
Is now *Pristine*
She's called Snow White
And *Sweet Sixteen*

I have a plan
We have to meet
Then she'll get peeled
In Bleeker Street
I'd slice her up
But I guess
That would leave
An awful mess

So I'll fix her
With something neat
Injected in
A *Bailey Sweet*
Then put poison
In *Priscilla*
It looks lovely –
It's a killer

New York, New York
O what a sight!
The Big Apple
Take a bite!
Have a look
What's in my sack
Would you like
An Apple, mac?

Lovely apples
To give away
I'm *Granny Smith*
Have one today
Cherry Pippin
D'Arcy Spice
Beverly Hills
All very nice

Red Delicious
Henry Clay
Autumn Gold
To give away
Wolf River
Tolman Sweet
Suntan, Rambo
What a treat!

Oh *Granny Smith*
I'd love to munch
On a *Puritan*
Or a *Pixie Crunch*
But best of all
Oh Granny dear
I quite fancy
A nice *Grenadier*

You recommend
A *Bailey Sweet*
Or *Priscilla?*
What a treat!
Oh my goodness
I feel sick
I'm choking
Please help me quick

◆ **EPISODE 2: RED PRINCE**

Red Prince
Red Delicious
Fancied something
Nutritious
Perry Russet?
Very fruity
But look at that
An *English Beauty!*

She's the apple
Of my eye
My *Hidden Rose*
My *Prairie Spy*
But I can see
An apple core
Stuck in her throat
That must feel sore

I'll place my hand
Just on her back
Then wake her up
With one quick smack
Cor! There it goes!
And that is how
I saved her life
She's breathing now

My *Summer Rose*
My *Billie Bound*
My *Maiden's Blush*
She's coming round
My *Honeygold*
My own *Duchess*
My *Pumpkin Sweet*
My *Pink Princess*

They got married
And moved on
To some nice place
Called *Alfriston*
They wrote
Apple recipes
And propagated
Apple trees

The Wicked Queen
That nasty thing
She did 10 years
In Sing Sing
She moved away
From Manhattan
And went to live
In Prestatyn.

The Elves and the Shoemaker – a story from two perspectives

This is a straightforward retelling of 'The Elves and the Shoemaker', where the narrative alternates between the elves and the shoemaker. In one school this was practised with two groups, one doing the Elves section and the other the Shoemaker section. Then the two groups came together and performed the whole story.

Elves

Poor Shoemaker
And his wife
They've worked so hard
All their life
They're very poor
They never fuss
They need help
And that's us!

Nails hammer
Scissors cut
Let's make those shoes
Let's hurry up!

Shoemaker

No money
You and me
No more work
Poverty
One bit of leather
Old and tough
For a pair of shoes
It's just enough

Stitch and sew
Heel and toe
Good fortune
Come and go

Elves

We work hard
We are elves!
We've got no clothes
For ourselves
We can tell you
Life is tough
When you're always
In the buff

Nails hammer
Scissors cut
Let's make those shoes
Let's hurry up!

Shoemaker

Look at that
The shoes are made
The customer
Just came and paid.
Well I never
Life is funny!
I sold those shoes
For lots of money!

Stitch and sew
Heel and toe
Good fortune
Come and go

Elves

Back again!
Oh yes!
Four shoes to make
Success!
But hurry up
It's past midnight
We must be done
By morning light

Nails hammer
Scissors cut
Let's make those shoes
Let's hurry up!

Shoemaker

With that money
I can buy
More leather
And you know why
More leather
More shoes
More money
Great news!

Stitch and sew
Heel and toe
Good fortune
Come and go

Elves

Back again!
Well I never!
Now they've got
A pile of leather
We'll make them loads
What a surprise!
But we must finish
By sunrise

Nails hammer
Scissors cut
Let's make those shoes
Let's hurry up!

Shoemaker

Look at that
Two little elves
They've got no clothes
For themselves
We'll make them some
That's what we'll do
To keep them warm
And decent, too

Stitch and sew
Heel and toe
Good fortune
Come and go

Elves

Just a minute
What can this be?
Brand new clothes
For you and me
Shirt and trousers
And a hoodie!
Let's try them on
Oh goody, goody!

Nails hammer
Scissors cut
Let's make those shoes
Let's hurry up!

Byeeeeeeeeee!

Sleeping Beauty – a Latinate version

This version of 'Sleeping Beauty' was written after a workshop in which there had been a long discussion about how important it may or may not be to literally understand the 'meaning' of every word of a story. 'Latinate' refers to the Latin origins of most of the vocabulary and the use of Latin phrases such as 'mirabile dictu'. The words are deliberately obscure but hopefully the rhythm is strong enough to maintain the storytelling process and for everyone to enjoy the music of the words.

◆ EPISODE 1

Now I pray for
Your indulgence:
I bring this tale
A new refulgence
The story does
Ameliorate
By using language
Latinate

Sleeping Beauty
One has to state:
Nomenclature
Inadequate.
Her soubriquet
Must be eschewed
For Catatonic
Pulchritude

Christening party
What a mess!
Twelve dinner plates
For thirteen guests
But what was
Extraordinary
They omitted
Crazy Mary

She received
No invitation
That was a family
Obligation
Her exclusion
Caused such distress
Families!
But I digress

Then she arrived
Unannounced
A malediction
She pronounced
When you're sixteen
Come what may
Prick your finger
Die that day

The party spirits
Dissipated
The atmosphere
Inspissated
There was utter
Consternation
Total Discom-
Bobulation

But then one guest
As we all know
Made a vital
Proviso
And what made
The guests all clap
Is that she did it
As a rap

This curse has no
Abrogation
I can give some
Mitigation
She will sleep
In hibernation
In suspended
Animation

Ha ah ha
Ha ah ha

One hundred years
Without cessation
To the spell's
Termination
By a prince
From this nation
Who wakes her up
By osculation

Ha ah ha
Ha ah ha

Oh yeah

◆ EPISODE 2

Prince Charming
Turns around
Feels the rhythm
Hears the sound
A magic rap
Now how come I
Can hear that now?
I wonder why

He checks the date
And then sees why
One hundred years
Have just gone by
It is her time
He can construe
Mirabile
Dictu – it's true!

He sallies forth
A brave explorer
Through fields of Rosa
Multiflora
Hacks his way
Through the Rubus
Species type
Odoratus

And there she lay
Quite insensate
His catatonic
Bridal date
He knows that her
Recuperation
Needs a princely
Osculation

Often there are
Certain dangers
Osculating
Total strangers
But in this case
One carries on
It simply is
Sine qua non

The malediction
Is revoked
Carpe diem
I'm just choked!
Post-osculation
Sheer elation!
Matrimonial
Inclination!

'Allo darlin'!
I do, I do!
Awake at last!
It's really you!
How long I slept
Just who knows?
Gordon Bennett!
Stone the crows!

My dear, desist
Please no attacks
With stones upon
Corvus corax
Matrimony
Honeymoon
Then elocution
Coming soon

I'm well 'appy!
I'm bewitched!
I'm in 'eaven!
Let's get 'itched!
His gifts to her
Were thirteen plates
One dictionary
Three aspirates.

The Bremen Town Musicians – a story of grey power

The wonderful original story concerns the flight of four farmyard animals who are at risk of mistreatment. They run away from their farms intending to go to the relative safety of the town of Bremen. Then, after disturbing some robbers, they keep their gold and their house and live their lives in safety and security, never actually getting to Bremen. This version of the story is a celebration of grey power and simultaneously a tribute to The Beatles!

◆ **EPISODE 1: THE BAND**

Donkey

Just because I'm
Elderly
The knackerman
Is after me
Ageism
It's sad but true
The farmer wants
Me boiled for glue

London Town
That's where I'll go
A street musician
Playing solo
A tourist sight
And what a hoot
A donkey on a
Silver flute

Dog

The same for me
I'm passed my best
Can't round up sheep
I need my rest
Years of service
No gratitude
That is moral
Turpitude

London Town
That's where we'll go
Playing as the
Farmyard Duo
We'll play the flute
And clarinet
In Leicester Square
As a duet

Cat

Now I'm too old
To run about
And catch the mice
I get puffed out
So the farmer
I can tell
Wants to drop me
Down the well

London Town
That's where we'll go
Flute, clarinet
And piccolo
We'll play andante
And con brio
Busking as
The Farmyard Trio

Cockerel

'Geriatric!'
They mock me
Just because
I'm elderly
But I can sing
So I could do
The music and
The lyrics too

London Town
That's where we'll go
Flute, clarinet
And piccolo
The Farmyard Four
Has now been found
And I can pass
The hat around!

◆ **EPISODE 2: THE ROBBERS' HOUSE**

Donkey

I'm exhausted
Hungry too
We need a rest
This house will do
Let's look inside
Now keep quite still
I'll put my hooves
On the window sill

They're all villains
Counting money
Eating dinner
It's not funny
We can play them
A clever trick
To scare them off
We must be quick!

Dog

Now I will do
What Donkey said
I will stand
Right on his head
It's a tricky
Thing to do
When your dog years
Are eighty-two

I really need
My walking stick
Since I have been
So arthritic
I have never
In all my years
Sat between
A donkey's ears

Cat

Then what I'll do
Is climb on you
An eccentric
Thing to do
For me it's great
As now I know
I'm conquering
My vertigo

And problems with
Mobility
Since I had that
Dodgy knee
Life's a struggle
I've been taught
And that gives me
Pause for thought

Cockerel

I'll fly up there
Then I'll be sat
Upon the head
Of that old cat
We're all in place
We must look scary
In the dark
To the unwary

A four-headed monster
With eight bright eyes
Now we'll give them
A dark surprise
OK everyone
Now we're a team
So after three
One great big scream

◆ EPISODE 3: HELP THE AGED

Donkey

They ran away
But were so kind
Because the cowards
Left behind
All that money
So I can see
A business
Opportunity

I think I've had
A great idea
A Refuge Centre
Built right here
Restore this house
Create a new
Farmyard Four
Campaign HQ

Dog

Then we can build
A conference suite
Where farmyard stock
Can come and meet
It will be such
A special space
A 'Reminiscence
Meeting Place'

Our new slogan
Our new plan
'Say No To
The Knackerman!'
Give some respect
And dignity
To The Farmyard
Elderly

Cat

We also need
As we all know
A Recording
Studio
Busking would be
Problematic
Now that we are
So rheumatic

So we'll record
Our own CD
We could call it
'Farmyard Free'
An album that
Our fans can get
Downloaded
From the internet

Cockerel

A new group name?
What have we got?
The Animals?
Well, maybe not
There's four of us:
What could be more
Appropriate than
The Fab Four?!

Our first single
Is coming out
It tells the world
What we're about
A fitting title
That's for sure
It's called: 'When
I'm Sixty-Four'.

The Singing Bone – a magical mystery tour

The very dark original version of this story concerns three brothers, one of whom is murdered by the other two. Many years later, a musician finds a piece of bone in a dried-up riverbed and fits it to his trumpet, whereupon the trumpet calls out the terrible story. The two brothers are caught and convicted of murder. In this story, which is a companion piece to the 'The Bremen Town Musicians', the music of The Beatles comes magically to life!

One hundred years
To the very day
That The Fab Four
Came here to stay
Campaign HQ's
Inspiration
Was a Centenary
Celebration

A street musician
Came to play
For the party
There that day
In the garden
Under a stone
He found a piece
Of chicken bone

A chicken beak
How right you are
As a plectrum for
My lead guitar
He picked it up
And polished it
Then held it tight
A perfect fit

But when the bone
Touched the guitar
We heard a song
As from afar
The bone began
All on its own
To play and sing:
A Singing Bone!

And then it moved
So perfectly
In timing with
The melody
A tiny dancer
Like a star
Danced the strings
Of the lead guitar

It was Magical
It was a Mystery
That chicken bone
It made history
And we were there
On that great day
As the bone
Began to play:

Polythene Pam
I Need You
Eight Days A Week
Love Me Do
Sexy Sadie
Hold Me Tight
She Said, She Said
A Hard Day's Night

Dear Prudence
Tell Me Why
All My Loving
Don't Pass Me By
You Can't Do That
Wild Honey Pie
Not A Second Time
Hello Goodbye

Across The Universe
Like Dreamers Do
And Your Bird Can Sing
From Me To You
Golden Slumbers
You Won't See Me
Free As A Bird
Let It Be

Chapter 7

New Versions of Stories by Hans Christian Andersen

New Versions of Stories by Hans Christian Andersen

This project began as a way of exploring some of the stories of Hans Christian Andersen. Holding up a book for the group – many of whom had a visual impairment – seemed inappropriate and exclusive. I wanted to extract the essence of the story and to retell it in a performance that would be accessible for everyone. Either by reciting the text or by performing it in call and response, it is an attempt at inclusive storytelling.

The Snowdrop

'The Snowdrop' uses contemporary slang and colloquial language.

So there I was
Blossoming
We all were
Cos it was Spring
But then this girl
Came walking by
She looked at me
And gave a sigh

What happened then?
Please don't stop
Tell your story
Snowdrop

She picked me up
I'd been found!
She pulled me
Out of the ground
Her lovely smile
Lit up her face
Then she took me
To her place

What happened then?
Please don't stop
Tell your story
Snowdrop

I'm a gift of love
She's going to send
In a letter
To her boyfriend
How I suffered
No one knows
First class mail?
Stone the crows!

What happened then?
Please don't stop
Tell your story
Snowdrop

He kissed the letter
Cried for joy
He looked at me
I thought 'oi, oi'
He held me close
And then, you know,
He kissed me:
Oh no!

What happened then?
Please don't stop
Tell your story
Snowdrop

They must have had
An argument
He picked me up
And then he went:
'I've had enough
That's it – no more!'
Then he threw me
On the floor!

What happened then?
Please don't stop
Tell your story
Snowdrop

So there I stayed
For hours and hours
By then I was
A dried flower
The cleaning lady
You'll never guess
She picked me up!
Oh yes!

What happened then?
Please don't stop
Tell your story
Snowdrop

Then she put me
On this page
I'm a bookmark
At my age!
How great is that?
I've reached the top
Because the book
Is *The Snowdrop*!

What happened then?
Just have a look
Read the stories
In my book.

The Emperor's New Clothes

'The Emperor's New Clothes' is set in the world of contemporary fashion: 'Ab Fab' as one school called it. All of the designer labels are genuine except, of course, for 'L'huomo nudo' (Italian for 'the naked man') and Casa Nada (Spanish for 'House of Nothing').

The Emperor

I need new clothes
I do my dear
For the catwalk
Show this year
Something bright
Yet light as air
So everyone
Will stop and stare

Giorgio Armani
Christian Dior
Nina Ricci
More, more, more

The Dodgy Dealers

The Emperor
So cool you know
Can't tell his Maska
From his Mambo
We'll make a mint
And then we'll scoot
Make him a designer
Birthday suit

Rei Kawakubo
Gucci, Prada
L'huomo nudo
Casa Nada

This year's design
See what we mean
So delicate
It's barely seen
And those who say
There's nothing there
Are very stupid
It's so not fair

Valentino
Coco Chanel
What do they know?
Who can tell?

The Emperor

I don't see it
Pretend you do
No-one will know
It's not true
Send my PA
She's pretty quick
If she sees it
I must be thick

Jean Paul Gaultier
Calvin Klein
Dolce & Gabbana
Mine, mine, mine

The PA

I don't see it
Pretend you do
No-one will know
It's not true
The colours – ooh!
Your new design
The way it's cut
It's just divine

John Galliano
Fendi, Etro
Gattinoni
They're so retro

The Audience

We don't see it
Pretend we do
No-one will know
It's not true
Sensational
Yet not too loud
That would stand out
In any crowd

Fiorucci
Anne Valerie Hash
Givenchy
Their colours clash

The Awkward Customer

I don't see it
And nor do you
I think you know
That it's not true
There are no clothes
The truth is out there
The Emperor is
Completely bare

Totally starkers
In the buff
And oh! I say!
Enough, enough!

The Princess and the Pea

'The Princess and the Pea' contains references to contemporary London – Bermondsey and Leicester Square, for example – and uses general contemporary slang. The London place names can easily be changed for other local names.

The Prince

I want to marry
A real princess
The Royal Family
And nothing less!
I've looked for her
Everywhere
From Bermondsey
To Leicester Square

If she couldn't kip
On one mushy pea
Then she's got to be
Royalty!

The Princess

Help me please
I'm soaked to the skin
Cold and hungry
Please let me in
I'm a Princess
A sorry sight
Can I shelter
Here tonight?

If she couldn't kip
On one mushy pea
Then she's got to be
Royalty!

The Old Queen

Royalty
What's that about?
Is she kosher?
Let's find out
I have a plan
So we can see
Just who she is
Really

If she couldn't kip
On one mushy pea
Then she's got to be
Royalty!

Under her mattress
Put one mushy pea
One tiny lump
She'll never see
If she can sleep
Then she ain't posh
And she's talking
A load of tosh

If she couldn't kip
On one mushy pea
Then she's got to be
Royalty!

Morning darling
Are you alright?
We hope you had
A comfy night
We're having lunch
So join us please
There's pie and mash
And mushy peas

If she couldn't kip
On one mushy pea
Then she's got to be
Royalty!

The Princess
I don't feel well
So no thank you
That lumpy bed
I'm black and blue
The moment that
I hit the sack
Something stuck
Right in my back

If she couldn't kip
On one mushy pea
Then she's got to be
Royalty!

The Old Queen
A real Princess
So it's true
It's wedding bells
For her and you
The happy couple
Come and see 'em!
And this mushy pea
Goes in a museum!

If she couldn't kip
On one mushy pea
Then she's got to be
Royalty!

The Red Shoes

This retelling of 'The Red Shoes' is set in contemporary London, although the place names can easily be changed to fit other towns. There is also a version for Brisbane, Australia: 'First a boogaloo at Coorparoo / Then a cha cha cha at Pinkenba / I did a conga at Yeronga / At Jindalee I did my knee!'

I could simply
Not refuse
I had to wear
Red Jimmy Choos!
Then some old geezer
Touched them twice
He spoke these words
And they weren't nice

Dance, red shoes!
All night, all day!
Dance all London
Come what may!

My new red shoes
They came alive
They danced a jig
And then a jive
Just take them off!
Throw 'em! Bin 'em!
But they danced off
With me stuck in 'em!

Dance, red shoes!
All night, all day!
Dance all London
Come what may!

First a boogaloo
At Waterloo
Then a saraband
Along The Strand
I danced a brawle
Outside St Paul's
At Pimlico
I stubbed my toe!

Dance, red shoes!
All night, all day!
Dance all London
Come what may!

I did a pavane
At West Ham
And a belly dance
At Petty France
A chaconne
At Kensington
Seven Sisters
Gave me blisters!

Dance, red shoes!
All night, all day!
Dance all London
Come what may!

Then a galliard
At Scotland Yard
A quadrille
In Notting Hill
An almain
In Chancery Lane
In Borough Market
I thought I'd cark it!

Dance, red shoes!
All night, all day!
Dance all London
Come what may!

My feet are sore
It's got to stop
Now it's cha cha cha
And a lindy hop
Oh Cobblers –
Shoe Repair
So can he help?
I'll try in there

Dance, red shoes!
All night, all day!
Dance all London
Come what may!

He cut them off
O happy day!
My new red shoes
They danced away
But I don't care
Just let them go
I'm going home
For physio

Dance, red shoes!
All night, all day!
Dance all London
Come what may!

The Snow Queen

◆ **EPISODE 1: WHICH HAS TO DO WITH A MIRROR AND ITS FRAGMENTS**

Kay and Gerda are childhood friends. A magical mirror rises up into the sky and then smashes. Something nasty is about to happen.

A looking glass
Come what may
Don't look at it
Just turn away
Devil mirror
And yes, it's true
One look at it
Will do for you

A heart of ice
Splintered sight
Bad is good
And day is night

Devil mirror
Smash and shatter
Spreading all its
Dark matter
Around the world
A cold surprise
Coming for your
Hearts and eyes

A heart of ice
Splintered sight
Bad is good
And day is night

Icy splinter
Like a dart
Makes its home
Inside your heart
Itching eyes
Have care
Feeling wicked
Oh, beware

A heart of ice
Splintered sight
Bad is good
And day is night

◆ EPISODE 2: A LITTLE BOY AND A LITTLE GIRL

Kay has been touched by bad magic from the mirror. The Snow Queen arrives to carry him away.

There's something bad
About to start
There's an aching
In my heart
And there's something
In my eye
Stupid Gerda
I'm off – goodbye

Snow Queen
Ice and frost
Take me away
Forever lost

The Snow Queen comes
In blue-cold light
Come with me now
Before the night
Before I kiss
Your life away
For forever
And a day

Snow Queen
Ice and frost
Take me away
Forever lost

Flying north
Out of sight
Knife-edge wind
Northern Light
Fog and mist
Shining snow
Frozen rivers
Screaming crows

Snow Queen
Ice and frost
Take me away
Forever lost

My Winter Palace
Do come in
And stay forever
Pale and thin
Bone cold
Winter season
Of the Snow Queen's
Ice cold reason

Snow Queen
Ice and frost
Take me away
Forever lost

◆ EPISODE 3: THE FLOWER GARDEN AND THE OLD WOMAN SKILLED IN MAGIC

The faithful Gerda sets out on her search for Kay. She is distracted and delayed by the Old Woman and her mysterious garden. She then continues her search.

The Old Woman

He is not here
Come in and play
My lovely flowers
Forget and stay
Taste the cherries
Have some more
I'll comb your hair
And lock the door

That's my story
Where I belong
That's all I am
My dream, my song

The Roses

Roses tell me
Is he well?
We do not know
We cannot tell
Down in the earth
Where we have been
He's not there
We would have seen

That's our story
Where we belong
That's all we are
Our dream, our song

The Tiger-Lily

Hear the drum
The funeral pyre
There she stands
In the fire
And as it burns
Is it true
That her heart's flame
Will perish too?

That's my story
Where I belong
That's all I am
My dream, my song

The Convolvulus (Bindweed)

In a castle
Day after day
There's a girl
Who wastes away
She looks upon
A single rose
She has a name
That no-one knows

That's my story
Where I belong
That's all I am
My dream, my song

The Snowdrops

Two little girls
On a garden swing
And their brother
Laugh and sing
Blowing bubbles
In the air
Happy days
Free of care

That's our story
Where we belong
That's all we are
Our dream, our song

The Hyacinths

Three sisters,
Quite transparent
In red, blue and white
Incandescent
And so they danced
In the pale moonlight
By the lake
A ghostly sight

That's our story
Where we belong
That's all we are
Our dream, our song

The Buttercups

Lovely sunshine
Early spring
Golden sunlight
On everything
Grandmother
Sits in her chair
Cheerful birdsong
Everywhere

That's our story
Where we belong
That's all we are
Our dream, our song

The Narcissus

I can see myself
Oh, what style
Such elegance!
A gorgeous smile!
On reflection
I can see
In a saffron scarf
Oh yes, it's me!

That's my story
Where I belong
That's all I am
My dream, my song

Gerda

Autumn time
I've stayed too long
In this garden
I don't belong
My search goes on
By night and day
Cold and tired
I must away

That's my story
Where I belong
That's all I am
My dream, my song

◆ EPISODE 4: THE PRINCE AND THE PRINCESS

A raven tells Gerda that Kay has been seen at the court of the Princess, who is looking for a husband. Kay is alive and apparently well. Gerda is determined to find him. She travels to a ghostly palace where she receives some unexpected help.

The Raven's Story

There's a Princess
Wants to meet
Someone to sweep her
Off her feet
A proclamation
She did declare
Speed dating
If you dare

Every danger
On the way
Brings me nearer
You each day

In the street
What a crowd
Outside they spoke
So very loud
But in the palace
When she was there
They lost their voices
And stood and stared

Every danger
On the way
Brings me nearer
You each day

Then he approached
This pretty girl
Seated on
Her throne of pearl
But he had come
Just to hear
Her clever words
He had no fear

Every danger
On the way
Brings me nearer
You each day

Now how shall we
Get you there
I'll ask around
So don't despair
If we go on
Then there will be
No going back
For you or me

Every danger
On the way
Brings me nearer
You each day

In the Palace

Your tale is sad
Now take the lamp,
Stay close behind
It's cold and damp
These corridors
Are dark and dim
Let's find the room
And go to him

I will find you
Come what may
Searching for you
Every day

Shadow figures
On the wall
Horses gallop
Hunters call
What are these things
Rushing by?
People's dreams
That fade and die

I will find you
Come what may
Searching for you
Every day

Oh! Yes, that's him
Call his name
Hold up the lamp
He's just the same
All this time
Now could he be
The one I look for
Finally?

I will find you
Come what may
Searching for you
Every day

From a golden stem
Two lily beds
One of white
And one of red
You have woken
Me from sleep
But I am not
The one you seek

I will find you
Come what may
Searching for you
Every day

This golden carriage
Our gift to you
To search for him
As you must do
So travel north
To find your friend
Your destiny
And story's end

I will find you
Come what may
Searching for you
Every day

◆ EPISODE 5: THE LITTLE ROBBER GIRL

Gerda is kidnapped by robbers, but the leader of the gang is kind to her. The Robber Girl tells Gerda that Kay is under the Snow Queen's spell and summons a magical reindeer to help Gerda continue her search for him.

The Robbers

A golden carriage
Shines like the sun
And it dazzles
Let's have some fun
Let's drag her out
She'll taste nice
Barbecued
And served with rice

The Snow Queen
Kissed him twice
Mind and body
Trapped in ice

The Robber Girl

They won't hurt you
Not on their life
If I get angry
You'll see my knife
But tell me now
Why do you roam
Around the world
All alone

The Snow Queen
Kissed him twice
Mind and body
Trapped in ice

The Wood-pigeons

We all saw him
As he stood
By the Snow Queen
In the wood,
As she passed by
We felt her breath
And all our family
Froze to death

The Snow Queen
Kissed him twice
Mind and body
Trapped in ice

The Robber Girl

A reindeer ride
If you dare
To her Palace
But have a care
Fly, fly on
Through arctic nights
To the land of
Northern Lights

The Snow Queen
Kissed him twice
Mind and body
Trapped in ice

◆ EPISODE 6: THE LAPP WOMAN AND THE FINN WOMAN

In her journey to find Kay, Gerda meets a mysterious Lapp woman who encourages her to continue her search for Kay on the magical reindeer through the land of living snow.

The Lapp Woman

One hundred miles
Still far to go
Through darkest night
In frost and snow
Ride the reindeer
Make no delay
Danger
Away, away!

Ride on, ride on
In snow and frost
To find the one
Forever lost

The Reindeer

All the strength
I have got
Can twist the winds
Into a knot
Can you give her
Strength unseen
To defeat
The Snow Queen?

Ride on, ride on
In snow and frost
To find the one
Forever lost

The Finn Woman

Much good
That would be
He likes it there
My sight tells me

Speck of glass
In his eye
Ice in the heart
A long goodbye

Ride on, ride on
In snow and frost
To find the one
Forever lost

But we both know
Don't you see?
She has more strength
Than you or me
Losing Kay would tear
Her life apart
For all her strength
Lies in her heart

Ride on, ride on
In snow and frost
To find the one
Forever lost

Living snowflakes
In the air
Of knotted snakes
And dog and bear
And porcupine
All dazzling white
In the Snow Queen's
Arctic night

Ride on, ride on
In snow and frost
To find the one
Forever lost

◆ EPISODE 7: WHAT HAPPENED IN THE SNOW QUEEN'S PALACE AND WHAT CAME OF IT

The climax of the story: Gerda's search brings her to the palace of the Snow Queen. She holds Kay close and as she cries, her tears break the magic spell. All is well. They go home together.

The Snow Queen's Palace
Walls of snow
Doors of wind
That howl and blow
A floor of ice
Arctic weather
To freeze his mind
Forever and ever

Meltwater
On the ground
Take me home
Lost and found

For winter days
My special game
Ice cold reason
Is its name
Shards of ice
Fit together
To make a word
To last forever

Meltwater
On the ground
Take me home
Lost and found

With those pieces
Do this for me
Can you spell
Eternity
I will give you
When you show me
All the world
All you can see

Meltwater
On the ground
Take me home
Lost and found

Gerda holds him
To her heart
His frozen mind
A world apart
And as her tears
Fall onto Kay
The evil spell
Fades away

Meltwater
On the ground
Take me home
Lost and found

Icy splinter
In the heart
Starts to melt
And fall apart
Tears falling
Wash the eyes
Clear the glass
Stop the lies

Meltwater
On the ground
Take me home
Lost and found

The heart is quick
The eye is true
Gerda, is it
Really you?
Where have I been
Alone so long?
Let's go back home
Where we belong

Meltwater
On the ground
Take me home
Lost and found.

The ABC Book

This final story, 'The ABC Book', is a light-hearted version of the original story of the same name. If it looks confusing on the page, all should become clear on reading it aloud. There is a version of the Cockney Rhyming Slang Alphabet available on www.cockneyrhymingslang.co.uk, but it is in prose. This interpretation takes the first line of the online version, puts it into a verse format and then adds a chorus.

When you know this ABC
You can rabbit properly

A is for 'orses
B for stew
C for miles
That's me and you!

D for nitely
E for brick
F for vesce
That does the trick!

G for sss
H – leave 'em out!
I for an eye
What's that about?

J for cake
K for tea
L for bet
For you and me!

M for Sis
N for lope
O for the rainbow
What a dope!

P is for mash
Q for lunch
R for Mo
Useless bunch!

S for you
T to go?
U for me
What do you know?

V for Las Vegas!
W for whatever!
X for breakfast
Well I never!

Y for Mrs
Zed for sleep
And that's the lot
They don't come cheap!

Conclusion

Grow your own stories

Many of the stories in the chapter entitled 'Stories from around the world' have been written by participants of one-day Interactive Storytelling courses. These courses can be easily arranged by anyone with an interest in storytelling, and they can be implemented with little or no cost.

In the first part of the day, stories were presented that have already been successfully used. Many of these are in the first chapter. The morning was entirely interactive, with a number of presenters demonstrating their use of stories with the participants. In the second part of the day, participants divided themselves into groups of four or five, and were given 40 minutes to adapt a story or poem of their choice into an interactive version. People who had a dual heritage were encouraged to suggest poems or stories from their non-English culture. The stories in Chapter 2 are the results of those groups' work.

After the course, people returned to their workplaces and were able to experiment with the storytelling material. At Watergate School (Lewisham), for example, one member of staff began to write her own interactive versions of stories already familiar to the children, and this practice then spread throughout the school. This has contributed to the storytelling culture in the school and, because interactive methods of storytelling need not include the use of books or pictures, it continues to be a project that is inclusive in nature.

I hope that the stories contained in this book will be enjoyed by others, and I also hope that, having read this book, people will be encouraged to go and 'grow their own'.

Bibliography

Ackroyd P, 1990, *Dickens*, Minerva Press, London.

Andersen, P, 1999, personal communication.

Auden WH, 1977, *The English Auden*, Faber & Faber, London.

Burgess A, 1982, *Here Comes Everybody: An introduction to James Joyce*, Penguin Books, London.

Carter A, 1991, *The Virago Book of Fairy Tales*, Virago Press, London.

Coles M, 2001, *The Bible in Cockney*, The Bible Reading Foundation, London.

Davies RT (ed), 1978, *Medieval English Lyrics*, Faber & Faber, London, p66.

Frank S, 2001, *Sea Chanteys and Sailors' Songs*, Kendal, Massachusetts.

Gardner WH, 1953, *Gerard Manley Hopkins*, Penguin Books, London.

Grove N, 1998, *Literature For All*, David Fulton Publishers, London.

Grove N and Park K, 1996, *Odyssey Now*, Jessica Kingsley, London.

Heaney S, 1996, *Opened Ground: Poems 1966–1996*, Faber & Faber, London.

Levin B, 1983, *Enthusiasms*, Curtis Brown, London.

Lindsay N, 1985, *The Magic Pudding*, Angus & Robertson, Sydney.

Lowes JL, 1978, *The Road To Xanadu: A Study In The Ways of the Imagination*, Pan Books, London.

Joyce J, 1971, *Finnegans Wake*, Faber & Faber, London.

Nicoll J and Nicoll A, 1927, *Holinshed's Chronicle as used in Shakespeare's Plays*, JM Dent & Sons, London.

Pellowski A, 1990, *The World of Storytelling: A Practical Guide to the Origins, Development, and Applications of Storytelling*, HW Wilson, New York.

Porter R, 1995, *Beowulf: Text and Translation*, Anglo-Saxon Books, Hockwald.

Pound E, 1965, *Selected Cantos of Ezra Pound*, Faber & Faber, London.

Rose S (ed), 1998, *The Book of Genesis,* Penguin Books, London.

Zipes J (ed), 1992, *The Complete Fairy Tales of the Brothers Grimm*, Bantam Books, London.